Mastery in Reading Comprehension

Mastery in Reading Comprehension

A guide for primary teachers and leaders

Kala Williams

BLOOMSBURY EDUCATION

LONDON OXFORD NEW YORK NEW DELHI SYDNEY

BLOOMSBURY EDUCATION
Bloomsbury Publishing Plc
50 Bedford Square, London, WC1B 3DP, UK
29 Earlsfort Terrace, Dublin 2, Ireland

BLOOMSBURY, BLOOMSBURY EDUCATION and the Diana logo
are trademarks of Bloomsbury Publishing Plc

First published in Great Britain, 2021 by Bloomsbury Publishing Plc

Material from Department for Education documents used in this publication are
approved under an Open Government Licence: www.nationalarchives.gov.uk/doc/
open-government-licence/version/3/

A catalogue record for this book is available from the British Library

ISBN: PB: 978-1-4729-8095-3; ePDF: 978-1-4729-8085-4; ePub: 978-1-4729-8083-0

2 4 6 8 10 9 7 5 3 1

Typeset by Newgen KnowledgeWorks Pvt. Ltd., Chennai, India
Printed and bound in the UK by CPI Group (UK) Ltd, Croydon CR0 4YY

To find out more about our authors and books visit www.bloomsbury.com
and sign up for our newsletters

For Sylvia Daphne Thompson, my aunt, who was an amazing teacher. She gave me everything I needed to love and teach reading. To my husband, Alpheus, and my children, Nathaniel and Aaron, whose endless love and support keeps me going. To my mother, Lois, who supported my dream to teach. To my father, Errol, who believes in me. To my brother, Darrick, who makes me so proud.

And to all teachers whose constant dedication to children inspires me every day.

Contents

Author's preface ix

Introduction 1

1   What do KS2 teachers really need to know about reading teaching? 5

2   The 'knowings' make all the difference – planting or activating background knowledge 15

3   The systematic approach to unpacking the KS2 reading domains 29

4   How to use standards to build comprehension questioning 49

5   Questioning techniques that build comprehension mastery 61

6   Key strategies for building mastery in 2a, 2b, 2c and 2d domains 79

7   Key strategies for building mastery in 2f and 2g domains 113

8   Book talk-ability sample lessons for 30-minute group reading interventions 123

9   Pathways for planning comprehension effectively with rich KS2 texts 137

10 Conclusion: Bringing it together 143

Bibliography 145
Index 147

Author preface

This guide may have taken one year to be written but it is based on many years of trial, error, research, improvement and positive impact on the pupils' learning of comprehension skills which has led to hundreds of KS2 boys and girls thoroughly enjoying every reading comprehension session I have been lucky enough to teach. Teaching for mastery is no easy feat and it will bring challenges as pupils really have to take the time to truly see and experience the finer details that makes a text whole. This will be new for many until, once embedded, it will feel natural.

In the meantime, I will continue to travel from school to school, teaching, training and supporting teachers from all stages, and harping on about creating probing child readers – not just for tests – but for truly enjoying and understanding the books they read. This renders exams a secondary task by which pupils of all abilities, social and cultural backgrounds, who have been taught this mastery approach, will be undaunted.

Kala Williams

Introduction

Reading is essential for pupils to gain access to other subjects and also for a deeper understanding of self and the world we live in. Reading creates avenues for empathy, human understanding, intellectual growth and stimulation. It is not only necessary for simply navigating our daily lives but for social justice and survival. According to the Department for Work and Pensions' Social Justice and Disadvantage Groups Division document, 'social justice is about making society function better – providing the support and tools to help turn lives around' (DWP, 2012). In many instances, school becomes a secure space where pupils can be given the chance to fulfil their potential often not afforded in the home. In fact, teachers continue to bear the brunt of the responsibility of ensuring vulnerable pupils (particularly those from socially disadvantaged backgrounds) have an equal platform to accessing life's opportunities. It is through literacy that many will avoid poverty and a disenfranchised adulthood.

Reading has taken on many changes in focus since the 'reading wars' of the 1980s. The Department for Education (DfE) has thoroughly improved the phonics focus of the primary classroom, ensuring all pupils receive quality phonics instructions to enable them to be early readers. However, the growing focus on reading for pleasure documented in 'Research evidence on reading for pleasure' (DfE, 2012) has thrown up a paradoxical state in the classroom where teachers seek to find a balance between pupils knowing how to read, enjoying reading and being able to demonstrate they are skilled readers of varied text types. Reading for pleasure is hailed as key to increasing attainment but due to the standardisation of practice, at the end of each Key Stage teachers are faced with evidencing how this has taken place in the classroom.

Overwhelmingly, reading for pleasure and a love of books should not leave pupils incapable of demonstrating their comprehension of texts in a way that is evidenced in sync with standards. The reading for pleasure culture of a school can often sway between being 'time expendable' dictated by the need to finish a piece of writing or other curriculum work, or 'sacred time' which must happen regardless of other demands. The attitude towards this is very much dependent on the individual teacher or the leadership of a school, whereas actual reading comprehension sessions are usually timetabled on a fixed basis. This book aims to provide guidance on how to maximise teaching time in order to encapsulate a balance between pleasure and attainment by providing clear systematic practice with practical strategies which will greatly reduce workload. Having worked in primary schools for over six years as a KS2 teacher, I have very rarely seen a cohesive strategic approach for teaching reading comprehension. In other words, reading skills still appear driven by loaded curriculum language with varying degrees of clarity around the steps needed for learners to achieve each domain area. This was my biggest challenge in reading pedagogy and many conversations with colleagues revealed the same resounding concern. The added pressures of the end of Key Stage 2 tests often result in teachers trying to plug gaps in comprehension by focusing on the main components of the mark scheme. The result is a less systematic approach which fails to incorporate the less frequently tested domain areas in a way that complements whole language comprehension. This often leads to a less creative approach to teaching reading comprehension and many pupils ended up being disengaged from what fundamentally becomes a testing approach rather than a teaching one.

It is often the case that reading for pleasure becomes less of a priority as KS2 SATs approach (more so than in KS1) and more of a 'when we have the time' occurrence by the pre-SATs term. It is a sad reality of the demands of a wide curriculum and limited timetable, as well as the other administrative requirements of classroom teaching across the UK. However, in more recent times, we can gladly attest to this as a changing phenomenon. The new National Curriculum (DfE, 2013) has placed reading for pleasure at the heart of its content with the overarching aim that all pupils will need 'to develop their love of literature through widespread reading for enjoyment'. It also acknowledges the types of reading that need to take place throughout a child's literary learning, i.e. 'to read for different reasons, including for pleasure, or to find out information and the meaning of new words'.

The ultimate reading paradox itself exists within the pedagogical self. According to the National Literacy Trust's recommendations in their *The Power of Reading* document (Lawton and Warren, 2015), the challenge to the government is to build on its focus on phonics knowledge and go beyond this in order to support teachers to deliver comprehension efficiently. Their two decades of research has noted that there are clear deficits in the practice of teaching reading comprehension, particularly in middle to upper KS2, which if not addressed will result in disadvantaged pupils being unable to close the attainment gap. This in itself carries its own amount of professional pressure not only for school leaders but for classroom practitioners. However, it is my personal belief that much can be said about how practice is taught during teacher training and how this professional pressure is handled in the classroom. Many teachers who do not consider themselves passionate or subject experts on reading struggle to actually invent or find strategies that work for them and their pupils, and often end up taking a bit from here, there and everywhere based on social media interactions and other teachers' claims as to what works. Social media is not always a negative go-to as many experts interact daily in this space and go out of their way to help struggling teachers find lesson plans, resources, book lists and jazzy ideas for day-to-day lessons or nerve-racking observations. This is all valid in itself but the underlying problem is that while the curriculum has dictated what primary pupils need to attain by the end of KS2 in reading comprehension, it has not given a single outline or inkling of how to do so. It is assumed that through our training or placements we ought to just know it and get on with it. Therefore strategies in reading comprehension are different across the UK, leaving professionals with a knowledge minefield that can work either way in terms of progress and attainment. There is very little to no cohesive pedagogical practice across the UK's primary institutions.

One clear reason for this is a lack of systematic structure that is mainstreamed as a pedagogical foundation for all teachers. Teachers have a heavy workload and it is really simple to reach out to a group of teachers online joined together by the sheer need of support, and get exactly that. There is great value in this 'what works' approach and it cannot be dismissed, despite there being somewhat limited research-based practice input to some ideas shared. 'If it has worked for x maybe it will work for me too' is a statement that teachers who are looking for answers will adhere to. Leading researchers in literacy such as Professor Greg Brooks from the University of Sheffield, Centre for Literacy in Primary Education (CLPE) and the Education Endowment Foundation (EEF) have clocked on to this and have made these 'what works' approaches readily available online. I have tried to make *Mastery in Reading Comprehension* a clear, accessible read that addresses several reading objectives with systematic breakdowns of the strategies key to the cognitive domains needed to achieve it (with as little theoretical rhetoric as possible) while still linking to the cognitive science underpinning the practical advice. This book is intended to be a practical guide easily followable by KS2 teachers across whole class and group reading practice using child-friendly language and proven strategies designed for quick recall and application for all abilities.

Despite the focus on KS2 in this guide, it is important to note that a whole school reading culture that emanates from the point of entry and continues to Year 6 is essential and that the entire teaching community should be involved. The practices mentioned in this guide can therefore be easily scaled back and applied in KS1.

What is mastery?

Mastery as used in this book is the act of retaining, applying and manipulating various strategies which ultimately lead to a full understanding of what is being read. It is about developing the metacognitive muscle and stamina to deeply read challenging texts and a wide range of writing in order for the reader to demonstrate visibly what they understand. The aim of mastery is to develop probing readers who question what they read, seek clarity and achieve this independently. This book focuses on the *attainment* element of reading comprehension as one of the core outcomes of mastery. Attainment in comprehension is treated as a pupil's ability to demonstrate their understanding of a text through written reader responses. Mastery looks at how a learner creates links between questions, text and their responses to encourage a greater degree of accuracy as comprehension is made visible. The 'visible comprehender' is a term coined in this text to refer to any child whose understanding fully shows through discussion and ultimately through writing.

While this guide focuses on KS2 – particularly upper KS2 where attainment for transition to secondary school is key – many of the processes and strategies have been successfully used in KS1. The practices, strategies and results presented in this book have come from over four years of reading teaching practice across eight primary schools in the West Midlands, taught to over 500 pupils, the majority of whom were in Key Stage 2. These strategies moved 96 per cent of Year 6 pupils taught to greater depth standards and *all* of these pupils left primary education with at least age-related expectations under their belt. They are proven to work especially for average and advanced readers especially when used for both whole-class teaching approaches as well as intervention in group settings.

By sharing these methods with the wider teaching community, I hope that my contribution to the teaching of comprehension in KS2 will mean that there is more clarity in classroom practice, more rigour through a developed systematic approach and an unfettering of the cognitive domains of the reading curriculum. This guide is certainly not the only answer but will prove to be a pedagogically powerful tool for every KS2 teacher who wishes to develop mastery in reading comprehension in each child. I have trained many teachers in both KS1 and KS2 who have found my strategies transformative. I hope that this will be the case for you too!

1 What do KS2 teachers really need to know about reading teaching?

Reading teaching in Key Stage 2 makes one essential thing obvious – without pupils being fluent decoders of text, it is an uphill struggle. By the time pupils get to Year 3, it is hoped that they would have mastered the 44 phonemes in the English language necessary for us to widen their reading range even further. Without a doubt phonics is intrinsic as a building block to language acquisition but it is not the be-all and end-all (and no, this is not a revisit of the reading wars but a simple statement of the obvious). We rely on our Key Stage 1 colleagues to lay this foundation of fluency so we can plough through the complexities of the final stages of the primary National Curriculum. So – phase 6 phonics by the end of Year 2 is a must for us to be able to make our magic in KS2.

While teaching readers, all teachers must recognise that fluency is not only about automaticity of letter and sound recognition, it is also about expression and being reactive to punctuation and word meaning while maintaining a smooth reading pace. Fluency in itself is an essential pathway to comprehension (Rasinski and Cheesman Smith, 2018). A child who reads with meaning often demonstrates greater understanding of text. Therefore, it is important that we continuously work on fluency in all stages of primary school.

There are many things we may easily assume KS2 pupils are aware of in order to be fluent readers. We may assume KS2 pupils know when a sentence begins and ends. We may assume a KS2 child knows how to recognise a variety of punctuation and make use of this in their reading, e.g. through their intonation or their interpretations of meaning. We may assume a KS2 child knows what a paragraph looks like. We also might assume that pupils know that all things on a page are to be read. Experience will teach us that even in KS2, all of these are often completely inaccurate assumptions. Take, for example, pupils whose fluency is impaired by their own run-on sentence reading and monotone expression. They are not recognising the pauses or changes in pitch that ought to be associated with specific punctuation; they are also not picking up on the negative, positive or neutral tone of the text. How often have these pupils been given specific instruction to vary their voice? How often have they had this modelled to them? Likewise, many times pupils compartmentalise their learning but in order to master language, knowledge needs to be synthesised. It is therefore important that teachers model how multi-faceted fluency really is by effectively balancing pitch, clarity, enunciation and expression connected with the text content.

So, in addition to the components of fluency, what else do we really need to know about reading teaching?

1. We need to know the difference between reading for pleasure and reading for attainment

Reading for pleasure is very much about cultivating a love of books and is a principal driver for reading for attainment. It comes first and foremost in every classroom in order to get the most out of your pupils as 'visible comprehenders' of text.

a. Reading for pleasure is fuelled by diverse choice and enjoyment, driven by access and informal dialogue which gives the opportunity for pupils to dive deeper into understanding language.

b. Reading for attainment is fuelled by mastery which is a visible demonstration of a child's comprehension of the text they read, driven by explicit teaching of skills to embed strategies that de-complicate text therefore yielding a measurable standard.

KS2 teachers persistently seek to balance both and Upper KS2 teachers are often at risk of tipping the scale in 'favour' of reading for attainment as a result of the pressure put on them to produce data. There is no battle between pleasurable reading and attainment. In fact, both must be embraced as complementary for mastery teaching to be a reality.

2. We need to know diverse books by a range of authors

The Teachers as Readers research led by Teresa Cremin and other academics has pointed out the significance of 'teachers as readers and readers as teachers' (Cremin et al., 2014). Teachers with a wealth of knowledge of children's books make the best reading teachers.

a. However, where time is of the essence for building such knowledge (as is often the case) teachers can make use of the tried and tested book lists and book awards that come out cyclically.

b. Join book groups via social media, follow existing authors and publishing houses, read book review blogs and book recommendations avidly and keep up with new and upcoming children's authors.

3. We need to know our pupils as readers

Too often it is said that we don't have time to listen to each child read. This is a real hindrance to acquiring the full picture of a 'reading child'. Capitalise on every given reading moment in a week to listen to pupils read, even if it is only a few lines of a text as opposed to a long extract. Every listen gives a clue as to what misconceptions might be lurking when this child encounters words on a page. In addition to listening to them read we also need to know what makes our pupils read. In other words what their interests are what hooks them in and keeps them in that suspended reality. This is very much about empowering your text choice for teaching so that it is purposeful and impactful.

a. The reading for pleasure agenda has several ways in which this can be done, my favourite of which is the use of reading surveys. Baselining your pupils' reading habits is a very informative process and arms you with the knowledge you need to grow your readers. If done at the start, middle and end of the year, it also acts as a tracking mechanism to see how your readers develop over time (Miller, 2009, p.39–46).

b. If a child has been reading narrowly or only accesses books in school, these can be indicators that you need to stretch the range within your classroom.

4. We need to provide equal access to rich and diverse texts

There is no benefit in scaling down text for pupils who are working towards age-related expectations to access. In fact, you are doing them a huge disservice in doing so. All pupils need equal access to a wide range of rich texts and our effort should be in scaffolding our questioning and support in unpicking the language and meaning in these texts. By sharing the same text with all abilities, the collaborative learning is empowering and hugely beneficial for a child's learning development. Pupils sat in mixed ability groupings can participate in discussions and reasoning amongst their peers. Often those with weaker comprehension and word knowledge grow in confidence and understanding as a result. Hearing the language of rich text is empowering for weaker readers. This does not negate the necessity of intervention where decoding is an issue.

It is our duty to ensure that pupils are fully exposed to various cultures in books that avoid stereotypical roles. The CLPE's 2019 study into representation of Black, Asian and other minority ethnicities as main characters has shown that there is much work to be done in making sure that books that truly represent the world we live in are being taught in *all* schools regardless of race and culture dynamics. Diverse texts and diverse subject matters bring rich discussion, build background knowledge and empower all pupils to see each other as equals in a literate society no matter their differences.

5. We need to be aware of lexical grammatical complexities

To ensure the complexity of a text is well suited for your year group, look into lexical counts. Read up on Flesch reading ease score (see Flesch, 1951) and make use of the varied free software online that does the job for you but be aware that while it can help to make sure you are not using a text that is too easy or too challenging, it certainly does not take into account the nuances of simple language used complexly. In other words it is often not just varied vocabulary, a circa 1,200 word length or multi-syllabic words that create a challenging text, it is also an author's manipulation of language that is sometimes simple on paper but takes skill to access. For example: 'Sarah had a cheesy pie' versus 'Sarah told a cheesy joke' have completely different meanings despite using fairly simplistic language. Nuances or shades of meaning can often be lost when relying completely on Lexile scores.

6. We need to be misconception and strategy gurus

Strategies are a means to achieving an end goal. Activities are ways strategies are embedded. In other words we use strategies as a problem-solving mechanism when met with a challenge and we use activities to practise using these strategies. The only way we can build a bank of strategies is if we pay attention to the errors our pupils are making so that, with experience, you can predict the errors that may arise. I always raise an eyebrow when teachers say, 'oh we don't do gap analysis.' While a gap analysis is only a partial picture of each child as a *visible comprehender*, it will certainly inform misconception mapping in order to determine the priority of strategies to be taught. As such, knowing the errors our pupils make on the journey to mastery when trying to make comprehension visible helps us to predict errors, pre-empt strategies to arm pupils with and removes cognitive overload barriers as we are able to focus on hurdles and help pupils to overcome these.

7. We need to have a range of practice for teaching reading comprehension

There is no one size fits all approach. As a reading teacher we need to know whole class, guided, group, one to one and conferring methodology as well as when to apply them. Where whole class is the main form of teaching, being aware of the needs and progress of your readers will give you the intuitive jolt to scale down numbers and focus on specific areas of teaching which ought to be followed. You as the teacher know what is best and the classroom is your space to make the best happen. Don't ever be afraid to change the format used in a session or to request the resources necessary to do so.

8. We need to be familiar with and use standardised language in our questioning and text discourse

The art of questioning is key when encouraging visibility of comprehension. Many of us are aware of Bloom's taxonomy (Bloom, 1966) – but do we rigorously adhere to it? Often our questioning can riskily move between the tiers of the Bloom's pyramid and the consequence is either cognitive overload or low challenge lessons. We need to be aware that questioning is a skilful art which is layered, persistent, reactive and built to enhance textual understanding in its deepest form.

9. We must value practice as investigative reasoning followed by penmanship

Too often teachers encourage pupils to write something down in every lesson in order to 'demonstrate the learning journey'. My question is – who is this for and what is the nature of the writing taking place? Having reams of comprehension questions and answers in an exercise book shows me only one thing – you are testing instead of teaching. Pupils need time to embed skills and manipulate strategies in order to respond with greater degrees of accuracy. Mastery is when comprehension becomes visible in writing; mastery evolves from great time and emphasis placed on practice, investigative work, reasoning, editing and self-correcting. This practice is the learning journey to mastery. Spending time exploring a character, an event or a writer's use of language has much greater benefits to pupils fully understanding a text than answering several questions in writing from the get go. Hence, questioning takes on the role of a guiding tool during the teaching process rather than an instrument of assessment. We question in order to move readers towards independent learning by gradually releasing pupils from the scaffolding guided questions we provide (Fisher and Frey, 2008). We question in order to unpick thought processes, make errors apparent and get pupils to reflect on and re-align beliefs in order for them to walk away with the correct concepts.

10. We need to slow down, use less text and go deeper

The role of a reading comprehension teacher is not to race to the end of a book or a text. Certainly reading full extracts of a chapter or text is needed for pupils to form the big picture and gain context. However, when it comes to understanding how the big picture is formed, our job is to slow down and see the small steps that create the whole by zooming in on language in order reveal to pupils how words and symbols are interwoven to create mood, character depth and imagery. There is much that can be taught in a paragraph of rich text and much that can be learned from the illustrations in a book. By amplifying a significant sentence at a time, pupils learn the writer's techniques which they can also mirror in their own writing. It also reveals to us deeper misconceptions that can be tackled in order to make the rest of that child's reading journey a less troubled one.

11. We must read ahead of the class

It is kind of stating the obvious – but yes, I have seen it where teachers pick up other colleague's planning because they plan literacy this week or where PowerPoints or comprehension exercises are taken off a resources page and run with because time just didn't allow pre-reading or tweaking. So of course where this happens, expect it to not quite go to plan. For our teaching to be purpose driven and quality first (and all that jazz) we do intrinsically know we ought not to do this. So I'm not going to be condescending and go on about it. We are trained professionals bringing a wealth of skills to the table so let us be prepared for every moment we spend with the pupils we teach. It isn't always possible to read the entire book ahead of the class but certainly read a few chapters ahead and definitely read the synopsis of a text, find a book review written by other teachers, check out the author and illustrator. This will greatly influence your own ability to guide pupils through the text.

12. Use the Eight Wonders of Teaching as an audit for outstanding reading teaching

I created this doodle after observing 120 reading sessions across primary year groups. Essentially if all these are covered in a session, reading teaching is happening proactively.

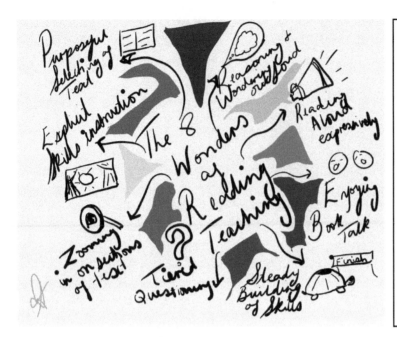

Figure 1: *The Eight Wonders of Reading Teaching sketchnote*

Purposeful selection of text

Text selection is all about what you wish to achieve as teachable moments: what you want the pupils to learn as well as what you know your pupils will enjoy. When looking into a text do your **RPAF** audit!

R – Reason		
Significant calendar event, e.g. World War 2 anniversary	Broader curriculum theme link e.g. focus on survival and resilience	Priority skill teaching, e.g. lots of opportunity for higher level vocabulary exploration, inference and language structure
P – Pleasure benefits		
A class favourite genre or a widening of genres, e.g. graphic novels due to surveying being the least explored text type	Opportunities to read continuously throughout the day, e.g. carrying on from comprehension focus	Intertextual links, e.g. books by familiar authors to inspire further reading or books in a series to tempt pupils to read more
A – Aloud moments		
Character voices and actions, e.g. modelling emotions with varied synonyms for 'said'	Rhythmical and engaging language, e.g. poetic verses or emotive dialogue	Key moments within 10 minutes to suspend reading, e.g. opportunities for 'what next' tempting or 'aha' moments to explore
F – Fluency practice		
Opportunities for acting out, e.g. particular character dialogues or actions	Repetitive lines, e.g. encouraging choral reading for fluency	Word play used, e.g. puns, idioms or sarcasm

Reasoning and wondering aloud

Reasoning and wondering aloud is a completely different element to the read aloud process. It is reasoning and wondering aloud by the reading mentor which makes comprehension visible to the child and **should not be confused with reading aloud or be done at the same time**. There are three perspectives teachers can approach this with: the characters' thoughts, the writers' thoughts and the readers' thoughts. All these 'voices' sound different, provoke different exploratory questions and reveal to pupils the layered unpicking often needed to gain the full picture of a text. 'Reasoning and wondering' as a character is very much about empathy and placing oneself in the character's shoes and it often pulls on both forward and backward inference skills. 'Reasoning and wondering' as a writer is very much about being aware of the writer's purpose or influence for writing a text, therefore focusing on contextualising language. 'Reasoning and wondering' as a reader is very much about reflecting on what may confuse or what has been revealed and therefore reshaped in the reader's imagination, and must mirror predictively the mind of a child reader. All 'reasoning and wondering' must be modelled by the teacher then followed by responses from the pupils, with open discussions about the suitability of responses dependent on the pupils' ability to justify their answers.

Reasoning and wondering as a character		
Questioning the actions or events around the character, e.g. I wonder why Lois walked away from me? What do you think the reason is?	Questioning what a character will do next, e.g. Do you think Troy will marry Helen after what we have just read? What did Troy do or say that makes you think this?	Questioning what a character feels, e.g. I wonder how Aaron felt when his teacher placed his medal on the shelf in front of the class? Why do you think he was grinning broadly?
Reasoning and wondering as the writer		
Questioning the purpose of the genre, e.g. Why do you think Shakespeare wrote so many plays?	Questioning the structure of the text, e.g. Why has the writer used this illustration? What does it show you?	Questioning the tone of the text, e.g. How does the writer's use of this phrase… make you feel? What exact word in this sentence makes you feel nervous?
Reasoning and wondering as the reader		
Questioning the meaning of words or phrases, e.g. This word… where have we seen it before and what does it mean? I wonder what the phrase… means?	Questioning own understanding, e.g. I think this means … do you think I am correct? Why or why not?	Questioning previous understanding, e.g. Oh! I thought this was because… but now I think it is… Do you agree or disagree? What do you think made me change my mind?

Reading aloud

Reading aloud is an opportunity to demonstrate fluency while also helping listeners to make meaning. It is often the case that teachers allow pupils to read along while they read aloud which is fine, however a much better experience is for pupils to completely observe and absorb all elements of the read aloud process. Most often I tell pupils to stop and watch with sticky eyes and ears while I read aloud which means they miss nothing. 'Deliberately *not* stopping reading the book to ask what we thought of it, why did that happen or what does it really mean is an effective way to allow pupils to think their own thoughts' (Pieper, 2016, p.134). I completely agree with this. Reading aloud is a magical time which is about suspending reality and bringing language to life while setting the tone of your lesson to come.

I find that read alouds tend to work best if they last no longer than 10 to 15 minutes, following which there is ample opportunity for pupils to re-read or even read aloud themselves while we work through comprehension strategies and responses to questioning. Reading aloud is your time as the reading mentor to show accurate decoding skills and demonstrate what can be done with tricky words, e.g. segmenting and blending or re-reading for accuracy and flow. It is useful to show pupils that often an initial reading of a sentence or a word may not yield immediate understanding and that re-reading is an intrinsic habit that readers ought to develop in order to improve fluency. Additionally, there is nothing more disarming than a monotone reader. As teachers, we must show pupils how to avoid this by connecting voice with meaning which yields appropriate expression and pitch. Incorporating gesticulation in the read aloud process is about meaning making. This is not something pupils may necessarily do but it will certainly spark memory of vocabulary and meaning. Many studies have shown that acting out meaning is an effective way to move learning from short-term into long-term memory.

Expression		
Voice variations that consistently mark different characters, e.g. accents, tone, speech patterns.	Facial expressions that reveal character emotions, e.g. demonstrating 'said' words or descriptive phrases while reading.	Pauses to mark punctuation and to add meaning to descriptions, e.g. He waited in silence, (pause) knowing this was the end.
Action		
Body language to reflect the mood of the text, e.g. upright and straight if a character is feeling proud or slouched and droopy if a character is feeling hopeless.	Acting out verbs while reading, e.g. pacing if the text says the character was doing so or waving your arms furiously.	Gesticulation is particularly useful for emphasis in emotive prose or streams of consciousness, e.g. poetry or speeches.
Pitch		
Clear enunciation is key, especially when reading unfamiliar words. It helps decoders, e.g. not covering lips while reading assists EAL readers, who often lip read to learn English.	Matching the mood is essential to help pupils pick up on when the language changes the atmosphere of the text., e.g. high pitched voices are more appropriate for happy or exciting moments, neutral tones are appropriate for the narrator's voice or side-lines while deep and low tones are appropriate for gloomy or tense moods.	Pace is very much a part of your pitch as reading loudly and quickly is scientifically proven to affect focus negatively. Stick to a medium volume just above speaking levels and a medium pace only slowing or quickening if done to demonstrate an appropriate emotion for a character's speech or actions.

Enjoying book talk

The principles of book talk in this book are based on 'wondery' (not enquiry) and exploration, discovery and revelation, re-alignment and re-visiting, summarising and re-telling. Aidan Chambers speaks of the informality of book talk as a type of 'gossip' without teacher impositions (Chambers, 2011, p.78). However, I think this may over-simplify the significance of it. The role of the teacher is to entice and engage; doing this informally, without any demands that pupils follow through with an activity, is about building a heartfelt connection between readers and books. It certainly isn't about imposing but levelling the playing field to an extent. The relationship teachers build through book talk leads to pupils being able to more critically choose and discuss meaning in text. Book oracy is very much a deep part of comprehension and asking questions is not a demand for an answer in book talk but certainly an opening up of pathways of thought and an invitation into seeking more 'tasty' bits to read.

Donalyn Miller speaks quite frankly about the 'slippery slopes of book talk' (Miller, 2009, pp.136–137) once formalised. Nobody likes being forced to stand centre stage and talk in depth about what they liked or didn't like about a book. Removing the pressure and expectations enables fluid and natural discussions to yield much fruit. Aha! and quizzical moments are a great way to ping pong conversation between pupils and teacher. The result is they look forward to more of the text and are often tempted to read the books you recommend by themselves. Teresa Cremin et al describe this process of reciprocity as 'a reshaping of traditional … boundaries' (Cremin et al, 2014, p.77). With this in mind, rather than book talk as a stand-alone session where 'speaking and listening' is an assessment point (therefore it is no longer informal) use this gem throughout reading comprehension sessions as a way to balance and revisit the relationship between the text and the reader as well as the relationship between readers (including the teacher who is equally affected by text). This is referred to in this guide as book 'talkability' which is a fusion of informal book talk and more structured reasoning around book content. Modelling quality book talk is essential and this is the extent of teacher-led involvement. This is also temporary as when pupils are shown how to meaningfully discuss text they become proficient at it. As the moment presents itself, speaking freely about books being read, other books called to mind while reading or sharing images in a book that made you wonder or feel an emotion makes 'teacher as a reader' a visible and entrenched part of reading in the classroom. Your job is to impart a burning desire to share or partake of what you have read and book talk will do this. The beauty of this is that you become more human and known to each other and this is a wonderful thing.

We need to know that the National Curriculum reading domains are loaded

Therefore it is our job to unpick them. One of the biggest challenges is subject knowledge. We often bring our personal emotions to a subject based on past experiences from our own education. While many teachers may not personally have enjoyed reading comprehension, to teach reading comprehension well for mastery, we need to develop sound subject knowledge and bring passion into the imparting of such knowledge. The reading domains are given to us by the National Curriculum, but what do they mean and how do they relate to the broader objectives in the English curriculum programme for KS2? There are in fact several steps involved in each domain area which can be made apparent. Many also believe that reading domains cannot be taught systematically. I argue otherwise and have proven that a systematic approach is in fact necessary to allow pupils to build up the skills needed to demonstrate visible comprehension, particularly when a domain is being taught for the first time. There is also a wider systematic correlation between which domains should be taught first, next and so on. Of course, certain texts yield themselves better to certain skills however it is about purposefully selecting according to the skills to be taught and teaching them in a cognisant order. This is a key part of explicit teaching – systematic build up removes cognitive overload and fully prepares pupils to flourish when it comes to learning a new comprehension skill.

There is also a difference between testable domains and other learning areas in the reading curriculum which are as important to be taught and assessed. Essentially, areas of recital and oracy such as the preparation and performance of plays and poetry, the ability to read aloud with appropriate clarity, intonation and expression, word reading and monitoring of own comprehension, the art of discussion around book knowledge, reading for pleasure and recommending books as well as the use of dictionaries are completely omitted from the testable domains. Therefore, for the purpose of this book we will focus on the testable domains, which are the priority focus for demonstrable comprehension while providing links to the reading curriculum content which informs them. It is also important to note that no domain is taught in isolation. Reading skills intertwine, are co-dependent and often are tested alongside other skills when it comes to demonstrating mastery. Hence, it is important that teaching sequences reflect the natural relationship between reading skills by overlapping with other domain areas despite focusing on one specific domain for a block of teaching. We need to be intrinsically aware of what to teach and when.

2 The 'knowings' make all the difference – planting or activating background knowledge

Our classrooms are very diverse spaces. These tiny humans bring with them different experiences or lack thereof and this often impacts on their understanding of language. Each text presents the reader with a context of unique characters and settings or information which might be unfamiliar to pupils. Priming pupils is very much about arming them with the background details needed to access each unique context. The 'knowings' is very much about subject-specific knowledge which can be found in a non-fiction or fiction book. For example, if the setting is mainly a seaside village with vocabulary meant to paint a picture of this experience and a child has never seen a seaside, this makes it twice as hard for them to create a picture in their head that links to the writer's intentions and their ability to infer. 'Azure-blue' may appear very differently to a child who has never seen images of blue waters of the Mediterranean or Caribbean Sea. Without knowledge of World War 2 and how this impacted on society, words like 'rations', 'blackout', 'evacuee' and 'air-raid shelter' will simply not connect even after telling the pupils what these mean. Certainly in our teacher training we learned about the importance of Piaget's schema (Piaget and Inhelder, 1969) but that never becomes more real than when you are about to embark on a new text where you know the pupils are completely out of their depth in terms of the knowledge necessary to understand the meaning of the language. When teaching reading for mastery it is important that teachers are aware of the schematic links pupils will be making between the world they know and the world within the text they are about to read. Knowing your pupils is the very first step to pre-empting the knowledge necessary for pupils to grasp a text. This will have a heavy weighting on which text is chosen for the teaching of comprehension and when. There is a distinguished difference between planting and activating background knowledge. Planting knowledge is very much about what is new to the pupils and will need to be introduced – this will lead to new schemas being built as they develop as readers. Activating is very much about prior learning and bringing forward existing schemas to make or renew connections.

I always approach a book using the mode of 'think like a child'. The questions we should ask ourselves are based on 'what we know' and 'what we don't know'. It is important to note that these exploratory questions takes place in the planning phase of teaching reading comprehension and that the answers will vary from cohort to cohort, indeed from child to child:

1   Do I know anything about where the story is set or the type of people who are characters (if there are real references)?
2   Are there any new words I will need to explore or unfamiliar use of language (e.g. idioms)?
3   Is there a complex or familiar moral or lesson to the text?

4   Is there a link to other things I have learned through curriculum topics (e.g. history, geography, science) or is this completely new?

5   Is there an intertextual link I can make with other books read or currently being read?

6   Are there any others in the class who have relevant knowledge and can help me understand through shared discussion?

7   What would I understand if I read this section?

Using background knowledge awareness in text selection

One of the best ways the brain retains knowledge is through experience and since the teaching of reading for mastery is about applying knowledge through memory, prior learning ought to be capitalised on whenever a new text is about to be explored. For example, when teaching a book like *Empire's End: A Roman Story* by Leila Rasheed (2020) in Year 4, I notice the image on the cover of the book is an olive-skinned character with an aquiline nose and woolly hair. I instantly think about how many pupils in my class look like this – where is she from? There are laurel leaves everywhere and she is dressed in a toga and wears an expression of longing. I see that the text belongs to a series called Voices which are about different characters' untold stories from different cultures. While reading through the text I scribble down links to potential prior knowledge or key knowledge I want the pupils to identify and retain such as references to Greek culture and religion, geographical references linked to Britain, Libya, Africa, historical and societal references to ancient Rome, life on the sea, Latin and Greek language. While doing so I note vocabulary I wish to explore from the first five chapters as well as new and technical vocabulary I wish to prime. This includes words on their own and groups of words that may be tricky for the pupils in my class to grasp, noting there are several loaded phrases referring to class and gender distinctions common at the time.

I also notice that the themes of isolation, social division, feminine strength, early maturity and difficult journeys are recurring ones. Some of which will be difficult for my class to grasp, with the exception of two of my newly arrived pupils whose backgrounds are remarkably similar (if in a different time of history) who may be very willing to open up in discussion if they connect to how I launch the text. These musings pre-empt any linking to teaching skills or domain content and are a necessary starting point for teaching any text. In the end, the text was moved to Year 5 due to its mature content and simply because the pupils in that Year 4 cohort were generally quite young. It is perfectly reasonable to make an assessment of the type of knowledge and discussions that will follow exploring a book and teachers must be confident enough to challenge the suitability of texts based on their own background knowledge of each child in their class. Recognising very wide gaps in background knowledge will remove the possibility of delayed comprehension teaching as you will undoubtedly spend more time explaining what and why things are than focusing on the text itself. What you are aiming for is a text that will layer schema, pull on memory and build on that through widening textual experiences. As the Year 4 class had previous experience with magical stories with supernatural themes it was easier for them to access my second choice of text so I could then focus on filling smaller gaps of knowledge in order to work on comprehension skills.

Once teachers have explored a text by thinking like a child, it is important to hook the text correctly, keeping in mind the key concepts needed to correctly understand it. There are many ways to do this. Some teachers rely on well put together slides with images and vocabulary, for example. However, I believe in a triangulated approach to activating or planting knowledge.

1   The first is based on 'what we should already know' – this is any reminder which pulls previous learning forward as relevant links.

2   The second is 'what is completely new' – this is about empowering pupils to access the text once reading by pre-teaching any unfamiliar vocabulary including technical words and exploring any new cultures or places.

3   The third is 'what can I bring to life'. This element appeals to my tactile learners. This is about bringing 3D items into the learning space or providing virtual experiences that can be adapted to prompt relevant enquiry and discussions linked to the text. Many times it is also about empathy. Perhaps the book deals with a difficult theme which you want pupils to be prepared to tackle.

What we should already know?

Often texts we explore share things in common with prior learning or even prior texts. The rich curriculum we deliver in other topics can serve to provide prior knowledge as pupils move fluidly through the UK education system. In saying this, what of the pupils who are newly arrived with no such experiences? This will need to be taken into account and providing experiences through use of images, visual media and of course discussion can help memory to be refreshed while simultaneously planting these experiences with pupils from other cultural backgrounds.

Where there are previously read texts with strong intertextual links either in terms of language or theme these always make good reference points throughout a teaching sequence. Background information already known does not have to present itself at the very start of a teaching sequence but should be interwoven throughout the sequence as the moment presents itself in order to reinforce the current learning. For example, when teaching the book *Street Child* by Berlie Doherty (2009) there are many opportunities to draw connections with the character Oliver Twist, the history of child labourers and orphan pupils during Victorian times and the origins of Barnardos pupils' charity which still exists. The essential question is: which of these links carries a familiarity and which is completely new knowledge to the class being taught? By starting with the new knowledge necessary to understand the book and its context there will be an essential hook to create a thirst for reading the text. *The Island* by Armin Greder (2008), which deals with difficult themes of prejudice because of difference, can be linked to *Orphans of the Tide* by Struan Murray (2020) and other books that deal with the topic of refugees. If these were previously taught, they can be recalled during book talk with the pupils in a way that makes themes in the new book accessible and comparable.

Essentially, when planning book progression, thinking ahead on the basis of intertextual connections increases text access despite variations of conventions or theme.

What is completely new?

There are significant things to consider when planting background knowledge that is completely new. As previously mentioned, it is best to be aware if the newness is too far removed from the experience of a class. Work may need to be done in other curriculum areas if this is the case and the text is compulsory. If the setting is based on a real place, geographical knowledge through images, maps and historical detail is very useful for contextualising a new book. Perhaps there are technical words used that pupils will need to be given the meaning of or, better yet, a familiar context within which meaning can be worked out. For example in the book *The House with Chicken Legs* by Sophie Anderson (2018) some pupils may not know what beetroot is and will not be able to imagine it in soup. They will struggle to pronounce Russian words like 'pchelka' and 'kvass' (p.13). By reading ahead it would be handy to guide pupils to Marinka's Glossary at the end of the book and to provide images where possible of the Slavic cultural references. Likewise, providing a simple picture would help them to grasp technical words as they appear in the text and to grasp any figurative references made about the information. And yes – I would do a search on how to pronounce words in different languages so I don't sound like I am winging it when I read aloud. The 'what is completely new' is an essential starting point. New knowledge is fascinating and acts as stimuli for curiosity.

However, the teaching of new background information should be made as real as possible by connecting with what is already known. In the book *The Unluckiest Boy in the World* by Andrew Norriss (2006), there are mentions of curses, a spiral image and lots of bad luck omens. By presenting pupils with images of a spiral staircase and a spiral chandelier we can begin to look at the meaning of the word and what both shapes have in common. When it appears in the book, straight away they have a schema to build on and can associate it with familiar mental images to grasp what the symbol referred to in the text looks like. Using downcast characters from other stories or media, e.g. television, can help pupils to start to understand the type of main character and what his emotional struggles may be. There is also the sharing of widely familiar symbols of bad luck such as a broken mirror, a ladder with a person underneath, a black cat and having a discussion about what these images mean and what they share in common will prepare pupils for what the book will explore. None of these actually give away the text in detail but entice and tempt pupils into the storyline armed with some knowledge about what they can expect. Before they even see the book itself, this preparation builds up a fantastic eagerness to read. Note that although the concepts or vocabulary in a book may be completely new, the trick is to link it to what is familiar in order for the knowledge to be efficiently planted. For this reason some may argue that it is always about activating background knowledge which then acts as a pathway to understanding that which is new.

What can I bring to life?

The use of 3D items can be a powerful thing in giving the pupils the 'knowings' necessary to understand the main events of a text.

While teaching the book *Holes* by Louis Sachar (1998), I wanted the pupils to fully understand how difficult the task was that Stanley and the boys had to endure while at the camp, so I brought in a shovel and we had a go at digging a hole in the playground – much to my caretaker's horror! The point is we didn't get very far before the pupils understood the sheer cruelty of the act and this simple but effective way of bringing the text to life deepened their joy at the moment our characters escape in the text. Now I am not saying go dig up your perfectly manicured lawns to make a point but think about what you can do practically that will empower the pupils with knowledge. Weigh heavily on the 'imagine it was you' instruction to pupils when you may be well aware that the imagining might be out of reach and think how you can make more difficult or out of the ordinary concepts in texts real for the pupils. Role play, drama and re-enactments as a part of re-reading are all techniques that can build empathy and knowledge to deepen access to a text – and that is straight out of the curriculum itself. Throughout the text we took great pleasure in chorally reading the lengthy hyphenated name for the pig stealing grandfather – with comical flair and a sense of 'don't care' mixed together. This drove home the fact that Stanley believed he was doomed to a predestined fate of bad luck and tumultuous times from his actions.

Language is also something that teachers can bring to life. By focusing first on technical vocabulary where meanings may not be apparent in the text or on complex vocabulary that may be unfamiliar it is important to place this language in an accessible framework or simply provide images that will help deepen meaning. Knowledge makes all the difference to grappling figurative language too. Predict whether or not metaphors will be missed based on limited knowledge and build the schema necessary to access it. For example, in the book *The House of One Hundred Clocks* by A.M. Howell (2020) there are references to various types of clocks, references to parts of England that are historic, foods mentioned that are purely British and even weather references based on English life – all of which are integral to understanding the storyline. For example, where the text says 'Even so, there was something eerie about his eyes that she couldn't put her finger on – like a slow-to-clear mist on a winter's morning' (Howell, 2020, p.57). In discussing this simile, I would predict that not all pupils may have observed the mist on a wintry morning and a simple moving image of this would prompt or plant knowledge that would lead them to understand the mystery behind the character's look, which implied he was hiding something and/or he was sinister. In order to ensure pupils are given the opportunity to work things out for themselves using strategies, the key thing to do is to first make visible the new language they will encounter in a mix of words and phrases, then to place these in sentences which enable them to determine the meaning themselves (where the words are not purely subject-related technical vocabulary). Then model or allow them to independently work out the meaning from the evidence surrounding the vocabulary. Once the meaning is determined and they are aware these words will appear in the text, check they have spotted this vocabulary and repeat the process to ensure the meaning making sticks in the new contexts.

Practical ideas to plant or activate background knowledge

There are two types of methods for planting and activating background knowledge that I have used successfully. There is the pre-read priming of knowledge and there is the drip-feed intermittent knowledge enhancement approaches. The pre-read priming occurs before a text is read and in some instances before a text is even made visible. The drip-feed occurs during readings and can often be unplanned as gaps in background knowledge appear. The bottom line is you can't always foresee each gap and sometimes they will be surprising. However, when teaching for mastery it is essential that when gaps occur it is time to stop, drop, discuss and collaborate before continuing with any exercise. For example during the reading of *The Star Outside My Window* by Onjali Q. Raúf (2019) it became apparent that pupils had no idea what the difference was between a burka and a hijab. A simple picture of both was flashed up on the whiteboard and a quick chat about the difference meant that curiosity was satisfied and the pupils had the correct mental images to continue to understand the text. What is important here is for teachers to also present themselves as knowledge acquirers and not the fountain of all 'knowings'. This also demonstrates to pupils that seeking knowledge while reading is a natural part of comprehension. It encourages questioning as well as self-monitoring which builds metacognitive abilities. Of course there is also looking to a thesaurus or dictionary but I have found these to be the least effective strategies. Dictionaries often lead to more questions that visual examples answer in an instant. The following are some activities used in the pre-reading or priming phase.

Examples of practical activities for building background knowledge

Silent annotation (What do I already know?)

Learning intention: To make predictions based on evidence provided
This activity should ideally be delivered after having taught pupils how to make predictions from a previous text.

What to do: Place at most five or six images related to the text on separate flip charts on tables with coloured felt tips. These images could include the cover of a book where metaphors are conveyed through imagery; images related to different traits of a character without giving the character away; or images related to a major event in the text.

Give each ability group specific colours to allow you to track and assess pupil input and responses. Add a question to focus annotation on each sheet, e.g. Which culture do you think this text is about? What type of person is the main character? What do you think is the main problem in the book we are about to read?

Pupils go around in groups annotating their responses in silence. You can choose to do this in a specific direction, stopping when each group returns to their original table. Give pupils around two to three minutes for each image.

Expect some degree of copying from pupils who are struggling with the skill. Your role as silent observer will be to assess those with gaps in knowledge while noting which child is truly using the evidence for their predictions and linking this to their own background knowledge. Reveal and collaboratively discuss the responses on each sheet.

Mystery in a box (What do you already know?)

Learning intention: <u>To use evidence to make inferences</u>

This is very much an introductory activity with a focus on building inference through predictions. There is more of an emphasis on symbolism and how this connects to prior knowledge. If repeated with several texts it becomes an enjoyable expectation for the pupils who can't wait to see what gets pulled out of the mystery in a box.

Figure 2 *Example of 'mystery in a box' items for historical Victorian themed text, including coal, a flat cap and a model rat*

What to do: Have some 3D items connected to the text. Think theme, mood and characters when selecting items.

If the mood is sombre or sad you could have bits of fabric or coloured cards with dull or dark colours. If the main character is adventurous then it could be an action figure with similar characteristics. If the theme is one of overcoming difficulties you could have another familiar book with a similar theme included which you can use to compare.

Tell the pupils there is a mystery around the type of text we are about to read and the box (I usually decorate this with question marks of different colours on plain paper for visual appeal) will give us clues to help us figure out three mystery elements. For example you could focus on 'what is the mood' and explain what mood is – that it is the emotional feeling we will get overall when we read the text. You could then shift focus to 'what are the main traits of the important character(s)' – get the pupils to focus on personality characteristics as opposed to the gender of the character(s), which will result in much richer discussions. Finally, discuss 'what is the theme of the text' explaining to the pupils that theme is about the overall focus of the text as a message for the audience. Give some examples based on books already read, being careful not to mention the theme of the text to be explored.

Reveal an item to the whole class then show it carefully to each table. Allow for much collaboration and discussion in groups.

How many questions? (What is completely new?)

Learning intention: To use questions to improve understanding

The aim of this activity is to bridge to gaps in background knowledge to allow for a more informed and enriching read of the text.

   What to do: Provide images related to the main setting of the text or items of significance used by characters. Make cards with technical vocabulary or unfamiliar language (these could be words or idiomatic sayings) from the text that you think may be new to the class. Provide each table with three images, two items and one card to be explored in groups. Ask pupils to generate as many questions about them as possible (either in pairs or independently for more of a challenge) on sticky notes, based on what they wish to find out. Pupils will then collate questions for presenting to the class (it is useful to nominate two from the table beforehand to share with the class on their group's behalf). The chosen pupils must present their group's questions. If any question is repeated, their group will have to generate a new one to replace one of the repetitions. As you assess what they are doing, model examples of great questions, you might generate as you investigate as well as highlight good questioning from the shared examples of the pupils. Try to give varied physical items and vocabulary cards to tables so there are new questions for each item in round one while keeping pictures the same. Stop and pick out the most intriguing questions you have noticed from each table. I tend to phrase it as questions I also want answered or questions we all thought of. Then circulate items in round two and repeat the activity this time with less formality – no need to replace any repeated questions, simply allow the pupils to monitor their own curiosity. You will notice as they share questions many will start to ask for repeated ones to be replaced with another without your input. Put each item at the front for a visual display along with any matching questions you have targeted. Read the questions aloud to generate lots of book talk. Work through answers to their questions with the pupils, e.g. new pronunciations, etymology of words, examples of how idioms are used and what they mean, the real life geographical location of settings and significant historical events or context which will appear in the text.

Match the images (What do I already know and what can I bring to life?)

Learning intention: To make links based on evidence and knowledge

   This is very much about pupils using their knowledge of the world to inform their thinking. Creating links is an intricate way of upskilling cognitive reasoning, based on critical reviewing of evidence.

Figure 3 *Example of 'match the images' activity – Year 6*

What to do: Use several pairs or groups of images that are linked in meaning or relationship. The images I choose are very specific without giving away the details of a text. For example, if the book is *Holes*, (Sachar, 1998), I might have a picture of a snake, a picture of a bite mark made from fangs, a picture of an anti-venom medicine bottle. This works well in pairs and all pupils can have the same images cut individually like playing cards. Pupils are to put together linked images and share why they think they are related. Do a wider comparison with the group and where there are differences, get pupils to reason why their matches differed. Interestingly, many times the varied background knowledge of the pupils will open up amazing lines of reasoning that enriches the knowledge of the wider class.

For example, in Figure 3, pupils are matching pictures related to *Holes*. There is an image of a water canteen, a boy in prison overalls, a photograph from the film of all the holes the boys dug, a shovel on the table, a photograph of the character 'Kissin' Kate Barlow' before she became a criminal and a wanted poster when she did, among other images related to the landscape of the camp where the boys were kept. The pupils made several connections and even matched the holes with the shovel. They could tell the environment was hot, dry and arid with dangerous creatures present. We then spoke about the fact that it was normal in some parts of the world for pupils to be harshly punished in juvenile detention settings. We discussed that sometimes they had to do manual labour using adult-sized tools. At the end of the exercise, they thought about how pupils would suffer with blisters on their hands. It was therefore no surprise when this came up in the book that the empathy was concrete.

Sketch what you 'see' (What can I bring to life and what do I already know?)

Learning intention: <u>To explain and discuss own understanding</u>

The use of sketching is very much about making comprehension visible and is an ideal activity after having read the start of a text. In other words, bringing the reader's understanding to life. What a reader sees in their mind can reveal details about background knowledge and is a key way to identify those pupils whose knowledge of the world may need refining or even sharing to the benefit of their peers. The collaborative learning in this activity allows for shared knowledge and an increase in metacognition in reasoning through understanding.

Figure 4 *Child A 'sketch what you see' example*

Figure 5 *Child B 'sketch what you see' example*

Figure 6 *Child C 'sketch what you see' example*

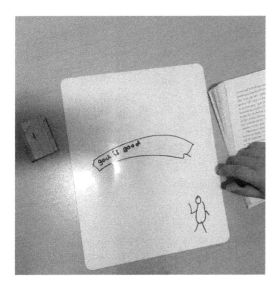

Figure 7 *Child D 'sketch what you see' example*

What to do: This is an essential part of assessing whether background knowledge is appropriately informing a reader's textual understanding and also a useful strategy to assess word meaning association. Select a section of text which is highly descriptive. Using whiteboards, pupils should draw what they 'see' in their mind as a result of reading the extract. It is important to tell them that it is a sketch therefore perfect art is not necessary. Deliberately choose those with misconceptions you perceive and get pupils to explain their sketches in detail and link to the text that influenced their interpretation. Use this key moment to see how each reader thinks. Identify best examples or where pupils are less confident, then reveal a sketch of your own based on the same passage of text. Link the text to the sketches, reasoning why these are *correct* interpretations – then hide the sketches from sight. Pupils whose sketches were accurate should observe a partner. Allow pupils with misconceptions to correct sketches based on what they now see. Stop the class and model questioning around what changes were made. Allow pupils to reason this aloud with evidence from the text. Where further refinement is needed model repeating the text and allowing comprehension to be reformed, e.g. 'Look at the text. Where is the lamp? Where did you draw it? Can you correct that? Highlight to the pupils that when supporting a partner it is important not to give the answer away but to always get their partner to re-read the evidence and think again in order to make a correction. Allow pupils with correct comprehension to act as mini-teachers and listen to the reason why corrections were made. Allow them to challenge reasoning with text evidence. Where possible support pupils by showing real life pictorial examples.

Take for example the sketches created by Year 6 during a reading of the text *Street Child*, shown in Figures 4–7. The quote focused on from the text was: 'There were four big arches across the ceiling with letters on them, and Mr Barrack would begin the day…asking one of the boys to read out the words…God is good, God is just, God is love…' (Doherty, 2009, p.52). During this reading I wanted to see if the pupils fully understood what was taking place before delving into the religious words. The sketches they produced revealed a variety of gaps in their knowledge both of the outside world and of vocabulary and meaning. Only a handful of pupils were aware of what the text actually meant.

In Figure 4, Child A had a knowledge of arches, directional prepositional language and the context of the setting. You can clearly see arches across a ceiling with words writing on them and that these were above the pupils in the classroom. This child did continue to draw a teacher pointing to the words and a child sat at the desk. I am now aware that this child has the background knowledge needed to access meaning and this knowledge was used to inform the class of the correct interpretation.

Child B (see Figure 5) understood the words were on the ceiling but had no knowledge of what arches looked like. However the child was able to understand the significance of the teacher making the pupils repeat the words and surely has an impression of the overbearing nature of the action by the size of the letters and the stern manner of the teacher.

Child C (see Figure 6) had very different background knowledge with several misconceptions which skewed their interpretation of the text. This child presented literal meanings and saw letters as actual post mail hanging from arches and clearly has a limited knowledge of what arches actually look like, having drawn them upside down.

Child D (see Figure 7) interpreted arches as one singular arch and became stuck when realising there was more than one statement. The gap in knowledge here was grammatical plurality and because they failed to recognise 'arches' as meaning more than one arch, comprehension was blocked and the rest of the mental image fell apart. After some time this child had simply given up, having re-read the text over and over again oblivious of the grammatical structure of 'arches'.

It is important to note that all of these pupils were in fact considered to be working at greater depth. This tells us one significant thing: each child's prior knowledge of language and of the world can have significant effects on understanding regardless of what they can demonstrate for mastery.

Who said what? (What do I already know and what can I bring to life?)

Learning intention: <u>To identify the theme or convention of text(s)</u>

This is about activating prior learning through memory of characters and their traits while at the same time sensitising pupils to the theme and potentially the convention of the book to come.

What to do: This activity is great for creating intertextual links. Use characters from previously read books or text extracts familiar to the pupils with a similar theme to the new text the pupils are about to explore. For example, if the theme of the new book is 'good winning over evil' – choose previous texts with the same theme. You can use a mixture of images and quotations. Start with a narrow range of images and quotations then build up to several pairs (no odd ones out).

Pupils are to match which quote goes with which character. This works very well with film or illustrated images of characters and quotes from the text.

Then introduce the two characters from the new book, ideally a protagonist and an antagonist, along with quotes for each. Present visuals of the characters (even if these must be sourced outside of the text), as simply giving pupils the name of the character won't work.

Pupils are to determine which quote goes with which character and reason why they thought this using evidence from the images to back up their choice. Generate lots of talk around characterisation, predicted personalities and behaviours and capture these on a display for revisiting later. Use your plenary to discuss what the pupils think the theme is of the new book based on the characters and texts explored in the activity. Add their suggested theme to the display.

Do not disclose if they are correct but when reading the text, allow the pupils to reflect on previous opinions and determine whether or not they were correct. If incorrect, they should explain what new detail made them change their original idea.

3 The systematic approach to unpacking the KS2 reading domains

As KS2 teachers, preparation for the SATs benchmark exam is one of our joys (nod and agree here). It is hoped that this chapter will shed some light on what the test really consists of and how this impacts on *how* as well as *what* we teach in order to fully prepare our Year 6 pupils. No – we don't teach to the test, but cognitive domains will be measured and unless we expose learners to the language and format of standards this will leave our pupils at a disadvantage when it comes to attainment. Let's not shy away from the inevitable and instead step into this exam business armed and informed.

According to the Standards and Testing Agency, the following are the testable reading domains for KS2 (STA, 2015, p.7). I have added their useful teacher-friendly abbreviated references in brackets as follows:

2a – give/explain the meaning of words in context (vocabulary and meaning)

2b – retrieve and record information/identify key details from fiction and non-fiction (retrieval)

2c – summarise main ideas from more than one paragraph (summarising)

2d – make inferences from the text/explain and justify inferences with evidence from the text (inference and justification)

2e – predict what might happen from details stated and implied (prediction)

2f – identify/explain how information/narrative content is related and contributes to meaning as a whole (content and meaning)

2g – identify/explain how meaning is enhanced through choice of words and phrases (choice of language and effect)

2h – make comparisons within the text (comparison).

Each cognitive domain features in the SATs test in varying degrees of mark allocation as outlined in Figure 8 on page 30.

Note the priority weightings given to vocabulary and meaning (up to 20 per cent of marks), retrieval and inference (up to 50 per cent each of marks) with summarising potentially accounting for up to 12 per cent of marks allocated in the test. While other domains feature up to 6 per cent each, this does not mean we will take them for granted in our pedagogy as they are equally important if mastery is to be achieved. The dilemma is ultimately which of the reading skills need to be taught in order for these cognitive domains to be covered in full. Reading skills are treated in this book as the mastery of a cognitive domain while strategies are the smaller processes necessary in order to demonstrate each domain area.

National curriculum reference	Number of marks	Percentage of total mark
2a give / explain the meaning of words in context	5–10	10–20%
2b retrieve and record information / identify key details from fiction and non-fiction	8–25	16–50%
2c summarise main ideas from more than one paragraph	1–6	2–12%
2d make inferences from the text / explain and justify inferences with evidence from the text	8–25	16–50%
2e predict what might happen from details stated and implied	0–3	0–6%
2f identify / explain how information / narrative content is related and contributes to meaning as a whole	0–3	0–6%
2g identify / explain how meaning is enhanced through choice of words and phrases	0–3	0–6%
2h make comparisons within the text	0–3	0–6%

Figure 8: *Profile of marks by content area with added priority weighting indicator (STA, 2015, p.12)*

It is important that teachers recognise that there are always two phases in teaching reading skills – Phase 1 being skill introduction and Phase 2 being gradual release (Reutzel, 2011). The introductory phase takes the view that the reader is being taught a skill for the first time. It relies on explicit teaching through heavy modelling and scaffolding through questioning in order for pupils to demonstrate their comprehension of the same rich text taught. The gradual release phase is about recognising when metacognition is at work effectively and pupils are independently applying reading strategies with a greater degree of automaticity, thus demonstrating their mastery of a reading skill. Phase 1 will demand a more layered approach to teaching within each specific domain with limited overlap of other domain content. Further, the teaching method of making comprehension visible through thinking and reasoning aloud will be a significant strategy employed. By Phase 2, pupils should be taught more than one skill as they organically develop understanding of a text, in order for several skills to be demonstrated at once. Additionally, the language of reasoning through justification will need to be evident both in discussion around text and mastery through written comprehension with little teacher influence. Figure 9 (see page 44) shows the systematic structure necessary in Phase 1 in order for Phase 2 to be more fluid and domains with persistent skill overlap to be achieved successfully. This structure is about building confidence and ensuring there are no gaps in the skills needed for pupils to show their understanding of text. The key step is to translate what the National Curriculum says about each domain and then transfer this into domain content knowledge.

Vocabulary and meaning

The 2a domain (give/explain the meaning of words in context) is connected to the following statutory and non-statutory statements from the National Curriculum in lower to middle KS2 (DfE, 2013) with further explanations added in brackets for clarification:

- *developing their vocabulary and the breadth and depth of their reading* (learning new words by reading widely)
- demonstrating their *understanding of figurative language, distinguish shades of meaning among related words and use age-appropriate, academic vocabulary* (show an understanding of metaphorical phrases or groups of words that imply meaning, use more advanced vocabulary than that known in KS1)
- applying *their growing knowledge of root words, prefixes and suffixes … to understand the meaning of new words they meet* (apply strategies of distinguishing root words from their affixes to help work out the meaning of new words)
- *using dictionaries to check the meaning of words that they have read* (independent use of reference texts to help clarify meaning)
- *discussing words and phrases that capture the reader's interest and imagination* (talk about language that affects understanding)
- *showing they understand what they read, in books they can read independently, by:*
  - *checking that the text makes sense to them, discussing their understanding, and explaining the meaning of words in context* (using the surrounding text to help make sense of vocabulary as well as using their own language to explain the meaning of words)
- discussing *language, including vocabulary, extending their interest in the meaning and origin of words* (through various mediums, including dramatic performances, to demonstrate their knowledge of vocabulary and its meaning while also learning new ones based on the history of word formation, i.e. morphology).

And by upper KS2:

- *inferring the meanings of unfamiliar words* (using the context of new words to clarify meaning)
- understanding *nuances in vocabulary choice and age-appropriate, academic vocabulary. This involves consolidation, practice and discussion of language* (demonstrating shades of meaning in their own use of vocabulary)
- understanding *what they read by:*
  - *checking that the book makes sense to them, discussing their understanding and exploring the meaning of words in context* (reading lengthier texts and monitoring their own understanding of vocabulary)
  - *asking questions to improve their understanding.*

It is not a surprise that such a huge chunk of the curriculum is attached to vocabulary and meaning as these are cornerstones of mastery in comprehension. For the testable 2a domain, readers first will learn to give the meaning of words and explain the meaning of words – both in context. This often is simply to give either a synonym of a word, words or groups of words through simple indication (i.e. circling, ticking or matching) based on use in sentence. Pupils may also have to explain the meaning of a word, words or group of words using statements in their own language. They will always be given a sentence or phrase in the standardised questions which demonstrates the vocabulary to be explained in context – so never vocabulary in isolation. This tells us that when exploring vocabulary it is imperative that the pupils see examples of how the vocabulary can be used in order to determine the meaning in their own language or identify an appropriate synonym. It also tells us that synonym words and phrases are acceptable as demonstrations of meaning.

The systematic approach to teaching vocabulary and meaning is split across both phases of teaching reading skills: scaffolded (introduction of new skill) in Phase 1 and gradual release (independent application of skill) in Phase 2.

2a give / explain the meaning of words in context

Phase 1	1. **I am learning to identify unfamiliar vocabulary.** This is about pupils being able to monitor their own understanding through questioning whether or not they understand, then annotating words or phrases they do not understand.
	2. **I am learning to recognise strategies for clarifying meaning.** This is about teaching and demonstrating varied strategies to clarify meaning.
	3. **I am learning to apply strategies to find meaning.** This is about pupils demonstrating and reasoning their choice of strategy in order to give the meaning of vocabulary.
	4. **I am learning to retrieve words for a given meaning.** This is about using the skill of retrieval in order to match definitions with synonym words or phrases given to the reader.
Phase 2	5. **I am learning to give words with similar meanings.** This is about indicating synonym words in order for pupils to clarify meaning effectively.
	6. **I am learning to link groups of words to a similar phrase.** This is about extending pupils' ability to give synonyms to the use of phrases for clarifying meaning.
	7. **I am learning to identify a word closest in meaning.** This is about identifying appropriate meanings according to context therefore overlapping with shades of meaning and some inference.
	8. **I am learning to explain the meaning of words.** This is about pupils giving their own synonym words to explain the meanings of words given.
	9. **I am learning to explain the meanings of phrases.** This is about pupils giving their own synonym phrases to explain the meanings of groups of words given.

Retrieval

Although retrieval in the KS2 National Curriculum is explicitly linked to non-fiction only, it is important to note that the testable domain identifies that this skill needs to be applied across both fiction and non-fiction. The 2b domain (retrieve and record information / identify key details from fiction and non-fiction) is linked to the following statutory and non-statutory statements in the English programme of study (DfE, 2013):

- *retrieve and record information from non-fiction*

And by upper KS2:

- *retrieve, record and present information from non-fiction*
- *The skills of information retrieval that are taught should be applied, for example in reading history, geography and science textbooks, and in contexts where pupils are genuinely motivated to find out information.*

Although not thus written, the ability to able to identify key details is actually an intrinsic step necessary for pupils to be able to retrieve and then record. Retrieving information is dependent on a child's ability to skim and scan. If a child is unable to determine what is important linked detail versus what is extra supporting information, retrieval becomes more difficult, which is where we see pupils retrieving far too much and creating vague responses. Therefore it is important pupils are taught to eliminate extra detail in order to focus on key information in a text without even being questioned about it before being made to retrieve information.

Skimming is the act of quickly reading – bouncing over words and picking up on key details such as nouns, actions and important descriptive language hence ignoring adverbs, some conjunctions and pronouns. In other words, skimming is about getting to the meat of the text quickly in order to determine the overall gist. Whereas scanning is usually in response to questioning when the reader is looking for specific information linked to the question asked. It is a deliberate search where many words or whole sentences can be ignored as they search for the key information. Finally, pupils will need to be taught how to record information by writing down the specific text required without excess or to paraphrase accordingly where finding and copying is not demanded.

The systematic approach to teaching retrieval would be as follows:

2b retrieve and record information / identify key details from fiction and non-fiction

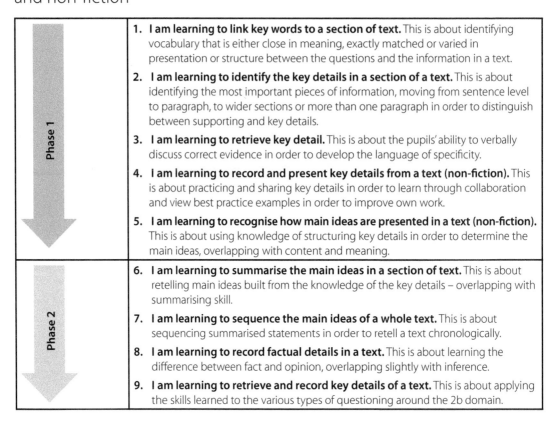

Phase 1	1. **I am learning to link key words to a section of text.** This is about identifying vocabulary that is either close in meaning, exactly matched or varied in presentation or structure between the questions and the information in a text.
	2. **I am learning to identify the key details in a section of a text.** This is about identifying the most important pieces of information, moving from sentence level to paragraph, to wider sections or more than one paragraph in order to distinguish between supporting and key details.
	3. **I am learning to retrieve key detail.** This is about the pupils' ability to verbally discuss correct evidence in order to develop the language of specificity.
	4. **I am learning to record and present key details from a text (non-fiction).** This is about practicing and sharing key details in order to learn through collaboration and view best practice examples in order to improve own work.
	5. **I am learning to recognise how main ideas are presented in a text (non-fiction).** This is about using knowledge of structuring key details in order to determine the main ideas, overlapping with content and meaning.
Phase 2	6. **I am learning to summarise the main ideas in a section of text.** This is about retelling main ideas built from the knowledge of the key details – overlapping with summarising skill.
	7. **I am learning to sequence the main ideas of a whole text.** This is about sequencing summarised statements in order to retell a text chronologically.
	8. **I am learning to record factual details in a text.** This is about learning the difference between fact and opinion, overlapping slightly with inference.
	9. **I am learning to retrieve and record key details of a text.** This is about applying the skills learned to the various types of questioning around the 2b domain.

Summarising

The 2c domain is about succinct retelling of key details. However, before a child can summarise more than one paragraph they clearly need to be able to retrieve key details in order to see how the main ideas are formed. When summarising is taught ahead of retrieval, pupils will struggle to demonstrate this skill. The 2c domain is linked to the following statutory and non-statutory statements in the National Curriculum for lower KS2 (DfE, 2013):

- *identifying themes and conventions in a wide range of books*
- *identifying main ideas drawn from more than one paragraph and summarising these*
- *Pupils should be taught to recognise themes in what they read, such as the triumph of good over evil or the use of magical devices in fairy stories and folk tales.*

Then by Upper KS2, pupils should be able to:

- *summarise and present a familiar story in their own words.*
- *[summarise] the main ideas drawn from more than one paragraph, identifying key details that support the main ideas.*

As you can see, by Upper KS2 pupils will need to be able to identify key details – which is deliberately pointing to the need to retrieve first so that they can inform their taking away of the main ideas. Although it states they will summarise from more than one paragraph, it is expected that pupils will then move on to the main idea across sections of text to demonstrate synthesising. There is also a covert link in this domain to sequencing a story and certainly in the testable domain of 2c we have seen this actively at work when it comes to sequencing summary statements in fiction and also in non-fiction. Therefore we teach this in both text types. If a child is to summarise and present a familiar story, it is obvious this must be done in chronological order which is sequencing.

The systematic approach to teaching summarising as a new skill would be as follows.

2c summarise main ideas from more than one paragraph

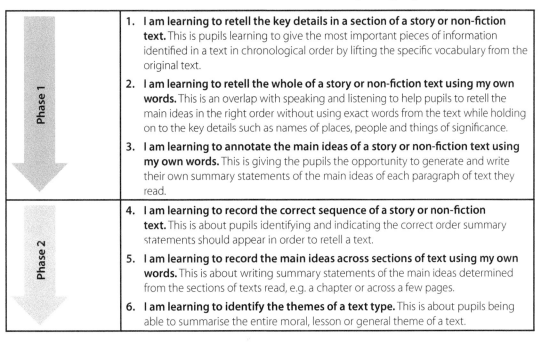

Phase 1	1. **I am learning to retell the key details in a section of a story or non-fiction text.** This is pupils learning to give the most important pieces of information identified in a text in chronological order by lifting the specific vocabulary from the original text.
	2. **I am learning to retell the whole of a story or non-fiction text using my own words.** This is an overlap with speaking and listening to help pupils to retell the main ideas in the right order without using exact words from the text while holding on to the key details such as names of places, people and things of significance.
	3. **I am learning to annotate the main ideas of a story or non-fiction text using my own words.** This is giving the pupils the opportunity to generate and write their own summary statements of the main ideas of each paragraph of text they read.
Phase 2	4. **I am learning to record the correct sequence of a story or non-fiction text.** This is about pupils identifying and indicating the correct order summary statements should appear in order to retell a text.
	5. **I am learning to record the main ideas across sections of text using my own words.** This is about writing summary statements of the main ideas determined from the sections of texts read, e.g. a chapter or across a few pages.
	6. **I am learning to identify the themes of a text type.** This is about pupils being able to summarise the entire moral, lesson or general theme of a text.

Inference, justification & prediction

The 2d domain (make inferences from the text / explain and justify inferences with evidence from the text) and the 2e domain (predict what might happen from details stated and implied) can be linked to the following statutory and non-statutory statements in the KS2 curriculum. Pupils should be able to:

- *understand what they read, in books they can read independently, by:*
  - *drawing inferences such as inferring characters' feelings, thoughts and motives from their actions, and justifying inferences with evidence*
  - *predicting what might happen from details stated and implied*
- *inferring the meanings of unfamiliar words,* followed by discussion of what is understood from reading. (DfE, 2013)

Inference and justification is perhaps the most loaded domain of them all. It goes well beyond just interpreting what the writer shows but does not tell but extends to what is implied by deliberate use of structure within a text as well as the nuances or shades of meaning of language chosen by the writer for an effect on the reader. The 2e domain (predict what might happen from details stated and implied) is often taught as a standalone area of learning which really isn't necessary. Prediction is a type of inference and should be simply modelled as a type of 'forward inference' (Broek, 1990, pp.438–440) pupils can make without further text to deduce from as opposed to 'backward inference' (Broek, 1990, p.433) where pupils have read the text and therefore are able to deduce from the evidence they are aware of. The research work of Anne Kispal gives further specificity to various types of inference. It includes 'coherence inference' (Kispal, 2008, p.2) where the reader makes inferences within a sentence level such as interpreting pronouns as indicative of specific characters, essentially occurring as 'local inference' (Kispal, 2008, p.3). Then there is 'elaborative inference' (Kispal, 2008, p.3) where the reader's background knowledge as well as emotional sensibilities embellishes their impressions to gain full understanding beyond the text which is really about 'gap-filling' their understanding (Kispal, 2008, p.8). 'Elaborative inference' is notably necessary in order to predict possible outcomes. The research also refers to 'global inference' (Kispal, 2008, p.7) where the reader infers the main idea or 'moral of a text by drawing on pieces of information' (Kispal, 2008, p.7). This study is very apt at recognising how many skills interlink to create a fully inferring reader.

A child's ability to elaborate based on what they know acts as a schema upon which they build forward inferences regarding what might be possible. Activating long-term memory is therefore a key element to open the pathway to inferring. However, within the skill of predicting, the possible is only part of the process of elaboration. It is the ability to move beyond the possible to the probable that determines a mastering of the skill of prediction. In other words, pupils need to be able to make predictions based on sound and justifiable reasoning.

In order for a reader to infer they first have to understand the meaning of vocabulary, the shades of meaning behind the choice of language and the effect it has on the reader in order to determine the text's mood. This is very much about picking up on how language creates impressions on the reader's imagination as they form a mental picture of the text content. Readers also need to be able to link the exact parts of the text that gave them that impression, therefore applying their retrieval skills when it comes to justifying their understanding. As justification is about proving understanding it is the ultimate part of demonstrating their mastery of inference. The major challenge of inference is teaching pupils how to structure their answers in order to explain – be it fully developed answers or simple succinct responses. There are three steps pupils go through mentally when being asked to infer:

1. Deciphering the meaning of language in a text in terms of what it implies and does not state

2. Gathering the relevant knowledge from their own memory in order to connect their own understanding to the text in order to hold a mental impression

3. Identifying the key detail or the main idea in the text as the question demands which supports their inference.

We can break this down simply into '**t**hink it' (think about the question), '**a**nswer it' (form an opinion), '**f**ind it' (find the specific text evidence that supports the opinion) and then be ready to '**e**xplain it' (give a written form of justification). It is important to note that different inference questions require demonstrating different types of responses for the **TAFE** process, which also has to be taught. The language of opinions is also a tricky one for pupils. When demonstrating inference it is usually around what is felt (evaluative) based on what was read. Emotive vocabulary is challenging for some pupils. Modelling as well as reading widely will be crucial in order for them to build up a repertoire of words to describe their impressions.

The systematic approach to teaching inference and justification would be as follows.

2d make inferences from the text / explain and justify inferences with evidence from the text

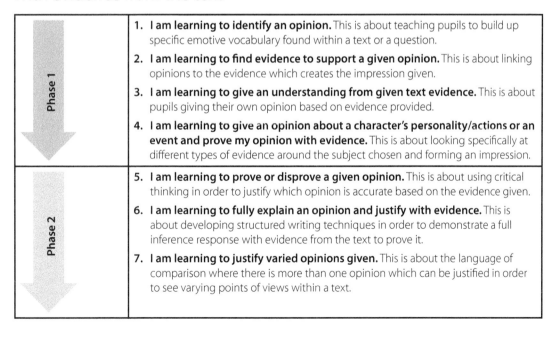

Phase 1	1. **I am learning to identify an opinion.** This is about teaching pupils to build up specific emotive vocabulary found within a text or a question.
	2. **I am learning to find evidence to support a given opinion.** This is about linking opinions to the evidence which creates the impression given.
	3. **I am learning to give an understanding from given text evidence.** This is about pupils giving their own opinion based on evidence provided.
	4. **I am learning to give an opinion about a character's personality/actions or an event and prove my opinion with evidence.** This is about looking specifically at different types of evidence around the subject chosen and forming an impression.
Phase 2	5. **I am learning to prove or disprove a given opinion.** This is about using critical thinking in order to justify which opinion is accurate based on the evidence given.
	6. **I am learning to fully explain an opinion and justify with evidence.** This is about developing structured writing techniques in order to demonstrate a full inference response with evidence from the text to prove it.
	7. **I am learning to justify varied opinions given.** This is about the language of comparison where there is more than one opinion which can be justified in order to see varying points of views within a text.

The systematic approach to teaching prediction would be as follows.

2e predict what might happen from details stated and implied

Phase 1	1. **I am learning to predict possible outcomes from stated details.** This is about looking at key details in the text evidence to give a likely prediction. 2. **I am learning to predict possible outcomes from implied details.** This is about looking at the implied ideas from the supporting key details to give a likely prediction.
Phase 2	3. **I am learning to justify predictions given.** This is about developing the language of reasoning where pupils have to provide evidence to back up predictions given. 4. **I am learning to fully explain a prediction and justify it.** This is about pupils writing structured responses of their predictions with evidence to prove them.

Content and meaning

The 2f domain (identify / explain how information / narrative content is related and contributes to meaning as a whole) is connected to the following statutory and non-statutory statements in the National Curriculum. Pupils should be taught to:

- [identify] *themes and conventions in a wide range of books*
- [recognise] *some different forms of poetry [for example, free verse, narrative poetry]*
- *understand what they read, in books they can read independently, by:*
  - *identifying how language, structure, and presentation contribute to meaning*
- *learn the conventions of different types of writing (for example, the greeting in letters, a diary written in the first person or the use of presentational devices such as numbering and headings in instructions)*
- [read] *books that are structured in different ways and reading for a range of purposes*
- *continue to learn the conventions of different types of writing, such as the use of the first person in writing diaries and autobiographies*
- [use] *non-fiction, pupils should know what information they need to look for before they begin and be clear about the task. They should be shown how to use contents pages and indexes to locate information.*

(Adapted from DfE, 2013, pp. 25–26, 35)

Content and meaning, in my experience, is one of the most underexplored reading domains in the curriculum. Most teachers tend to associate it with pupils being able to identify things like headings, subheadings, bullet points and captions. Generally, visual literacy also tends to point mostly at illustrations or images in a text which is, of course, crucial. However, there is far more to it than this. Content and meaning can be examined at the whole text level (how information is laid out on a page), sentence level (how information is presented in a line of text), word level (how words are deliberately manipulated in terms of typeface or fonts) and finally at the punctuation level (how symbols used within a text attribute meaning to a sentence or the entire text itself). It is usually easier to begin with the standard conventional ways writers present information for specific text types (such as letters, diaries, articles, newspaper reports, etc.). These are visually very different from typical narratives, making it easy for pupils to draw comparisons and hence pull out the differences they see. Poetry will show how content is manipulated into various types of verses and how this gives meaning to the message the poet wishes to deliver. By comparison, narrative texts require several layers of teaching in order to facilitate whole-text understanding.

There are many opportunities through both fiction and non-fiction to look at writers' deliberate manipulation of content on a sentence level. For example, some lines may not run in a horizontal left to right manner, e.g. a writer may use wavy sentences when referring to the rising ocean waters in a story or sentences broken across a page when the pieces of a vase shatters across a floor. Drawing pupils' attention to things like opening statements, footnotes or endnotes for extra detail is an excellent practice; you may also demonstrate how the reader knows that these exist by pointing out the number references or use of the asterisk in a text. Often these side-lined texts are ignored by readers despite containing significant information to enhance understanding.

On a word level, pupils need to see the varying uses of writing in all caps – as in not just for shouting or onomatopoeia but also for acronyms, for example. How often do pupils notice the varied uses of italics beyond the basic understanding of 'for emphasis'? If a writer deliberately shrinks, enlarges or expands a word, it is important pupils notice the difference and explore why it is done. Punctuation is a very important part of content and meaning. How often do pupils recognise that ellipses do not only serve as cliff-hangers with that ever famous 'duh-duh-duuuh' sound going off in the background? Certainly, in grammar they will note that dashes are an alternative marker of parenthesis, however in narratives they can take on the purpose of showing interruption to events or speech. How often do pupils realise that hyphens enable writers to creatively design words of their own in order to convey meaning? Do they really understand that an exclamation does not necessarily mean the character is excited but can signify an array of high-ended emotions depending on the context? Content and meaning is very much a part of a child's ability to infer on a local level. They need to see all of the content in order to draw logical conclusions.

The systematic approach to teaching content and meaning would be as follows:

2f identify / explain how information / narrative content is related and contributes to meaning as a whole

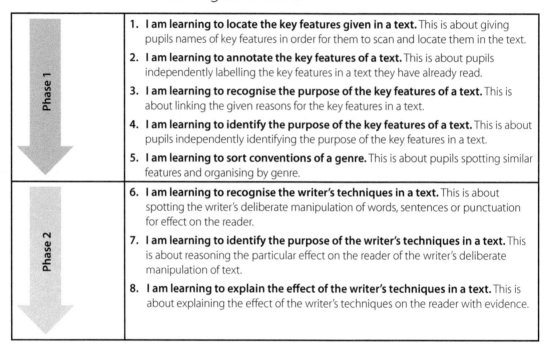

Phase 1	1. **I am learning to locate the key features given in a text.** This is about giving pupils names of key features in order for them to scan and locate them in the text.
	2. **I am learning to annotate the key features of a text.** This is about pupils independently labelling the key features in a text they have already read.
	3. **I am learning to recognise the purpose of the key features of a text.** This is about linking the given reasons for the key features in a text.
	4. **I am learning to identify the purpose of the key features of a text.** This is about pupils independently identifying the purpose of the key features in a text.
	5. **I am learning to sort conventions of a genre.** This is about pupils spotting similar features and organising by genre.
Phase 2	6. **I am learning to recognise the writer's techniques in a text.** This is about spotting the writer's deliberate manipulation of words, sentences or punctuation for effect on the reader.
	7. **I am learning to identify the purpose of the writer's techniques in a text.** This is about reasoning the particular effect on the reader of the writer's deliberate manipulation of text.
	8. **I am learning to explain the effect of the writer's techniques in a text.** This is about explaining the effect of the writer's techniques on the reader with evidence.

Choice of language and its effect

The domain 2g (identify / explain how meaning is enhanced through choice of words and phrases) is linked to the following statements in the National Curriculum (DfE, 2013, p.23, 26, 31, 34–35):

- *demonstrate understanding of figurative language, distinguish shades of meaning among related words and use age-appropriate, academic vocabulary.*
- *discussing words and phrases that capture the reader's interest and imagination*
- *understand what they read, in books they can read independently, by:*
  - *identifying how language, structure, and presentation contribute to meaning*

By upper KS2:

- *understand nuances in vocabulary choice and age-appropriate, academic vocabulary. This involves consolidation, practice and discussion of language.*
- *discuss and evaluate how authors use language, including figurative language, considering the impact on the reader*

- *be taught the technical and other terms needed for discussing what they hear and read, such as metaphor, simile, analogy, imagery, style and effect.*

The curriculum also makes reference to the use of drama in order for pupils to not only learn new vocabulary but also apply the appropriate expression based on the use of language. Oracy and performance play a significant role in the comprehension of language and effect. The opportunities for reading whole books aloud to pupils cannot go amiss when teaching language choice and its effect on the reader. Pupils should be taught that the language a writer uses is deliberate and purposeful. Deliberate in that the writer could have chosen several other words or phrases to convey meaning but has deliberately chosen the ones used in a text. Purposeful in that the writer's deliberate choice is intended to achieve an effect on the reader that brings together the full meaning they wish the reader to access. Often, modelling a text by reading aloud is a powerful way to open up a child's mind to the nuances of language and so reveals the author's intended tone. However, it is important that pupils are able to re-read the text independently. Essentially, this is about recognising that language can create a negative, positive or neutral mood. Negative language gives negative emotions to the reader, while positive language creates positive feelings. Neutral language is usually the language of fact – where information is stated in its simplest form with no opinions present. A statement like 'Mount Everest is 8,848 metres in height' holds no emotion – it is neutral. While a statement like 'Mount Everest is the most adventurous mountain climbing experience in the world' has an effect on the reader. The language here is positive by the use of the phrases 'most adventurous' and 'in the world', which give the reader the impression that the ability to climb Mount Everest is a thrilling achievement above all others. Teaching pupils shades of meaning is very much about them recognising how words can vary in emotional intensity of meaning in context.

Teaching shades of meaning is about making explicit to readers how language can move them into different emotions purposefully in order for them to develop empathy towards the text. It is the writer's role to paint many pictures in the reader's mind and the use of the vocabulary transforms these pictures into a kind of mental film. This film is filled with elements that appeal to the senses the writer wishes the reader to experience. By breaking down language into its positive, negative and neutral elements, the remaining job is to clarify which particular negative or positive emotion is felt and why. It isn't enough to simply say the writer used this phrase for an effect. It is imperative to identify exactly *which* effect it has. The 2g domain is very much a building block for a reader to infer and despite its minimal appearance as a testable domain, it should be focussed on when teaching inference as the grit behind the ability to determine language nuances.

The systematic approach to teaching choice of language and effect would be as follows:

2g identify / explain how meaning is enhanced through choice of words and phrases

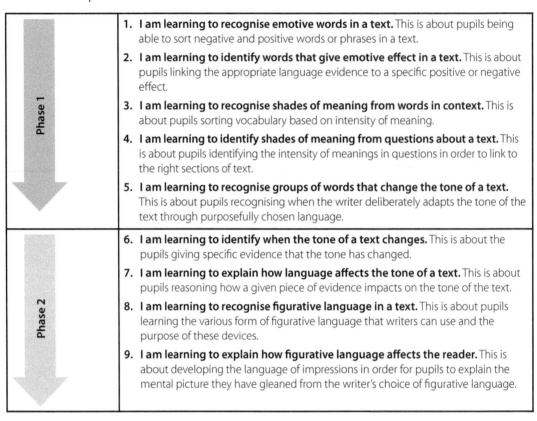

Phase 1

1. **I am learning to recognise emotive words in a text.** This is about pupils being able to sort negative and positive words or phrases in a text.
2. **I am learning to identify words that give emotive effect in a text.** This is about pupils linking the appropriate language evidence to a specific positive or negative effect.
3. **I am learning to recognise shades of meaning from words in context.** This is about pupils sorting vocabulary based on intensity of meaning.
4. **I am learning to identify shades of meaning from questions about a text.** This is about pupils identifying the intensity of meanings in questions in order to link to the right sections of text.
5. **I am learning to recognise groups of words that change the tone of a text.** This is about pupils recognising when the writer deliberately adapts the tone of the text through purposefully chosen language.

Phase 2

6. **I am learning to identify when the tone of a text changes.** This is about the pupils giving specific evidence that the tone has changed.
7. **I am learning to explain how language affects the tone of a text.** This is about pupils reasoning how a given piece of evidence impacts on the tone of the text.
8. **I am learning to recognise figurative language in a text.** This is about pupils learning the various form of figurative language that writers can use and the purpose of these devices.
9. **I am learning to explain how figurative language affects the reader.** This is about developing the language of impressions in order for pupils to explain the mental picture they have gleaned from the writer's choice of figurative language.

Comparison

The 2h domain (make comparisons within the text) is linked to the following statements in the National Curriculum (DfE, 2013, p. 25–26, 33, 35):

- *identifying themes and conventions in a wide range of books*
- *recognising some different forms of poetry [for example, free verse, narrative poetry]*
- *making comparisons within and across books*
- *have opportunities to compare characters, consider different accounts of the same event and discuss viewpoints (both of authors and of fictional characters), within a text and across more than one text*
- *be shown how to compare characters, settings, themes and other aspects of what they read.*

As a reading skill, comparison exists in the higher thinking area of evaluative reasoning in Bloom's taxonomy (Bloom, 1966). When pupils compare, they are examining critically, questioning and sorting.

Comparison is dependent on breadth of reading in order for pupils to build up experience. Without experience of variety, there is nothing to draw on to develop intertextual comparisons; certainly, without experience of varying characters or events within a text, there is nothing to compare. For a developing reader, we should begin by firstly by pulling on memories of similar characters or themes, enabled by visual prompts. For example, you could ask, 'Which other text uses heroes with castles and evil queens like those in the book currently read?'

Comparing different genres of text through wide reading allows pupils to distinguish between the varied conventions in terms of noticing how presentation and structure vary from one type of text to another. This practise builds up automaticity in identifying these conventions, which in turn builds up reader expectations in terms of content. A child should expect to see first person language in a diary entry or headlines in a newspaper report; they may notice when a narrative incorporates a different genre extract, such as a set of instructions, before returning to its regular narrative flow. There is definitely an overlap with recognising varying content and meaning in the development of comparison as a reading skill. Certainly, what is similar is the first normative way many readers make comparisons before delving into distinguishing differences which demands an even more critical evaluation, e.g. the question 'how does each character feel differently in the text as a result of the events?' is not so simple for pupils to explore when feelings are not stated but implied.

Comparison needs to be approached in small steps. Teachers should model the language of evaluation in order to train readers to critically explain. By zooming out from bigger points of comparison then moving into comparing finer details, the cognitive load is reduced. This develops a common ground of understanding in order for the skill to become more refined and to allow pupils to take on more substantial details. For example, readers often remember how a text or character made them feel before remembering why it made them feel that way. Emotions are one of the elements of human experience easily compartmentalised in the long term memory (Tyng et al., 2017) so when the experience happens again it is very easy for it to be recognised. Often pupils will easily determine that a book is 'good, funny, boring, etc.' and can compare this to texts that give them similar feelings. It is the detailed understanding of how each book gave these feelings that they will need to be taught to identify and explain.

It is key therefore for pupils to know the difference between comparing for identifying similarities and comparing for identifying contrasts in and between texts. Across more than one text, pupils can compare authors' intended tones (e.g. whether both authors intended to create suspense), authors' themes (e.g. both texts being about survival against the odds), authors' writing conventions (e.g. both wrote books in the style of diaries) as well as characters and events across more than one text (e.g. one character may have overcome a bully while one reacted timidly). Within a text, there are comparisons to be made between characters (from looks to behaviours), between events (causes and effects), between predictions based on characters and events (what they think would happen to this character compared to another character in case of an event). Finally, there is the simple language of which text was preferred and why was it preferred – where pupils have to employ the language of evaluation through reasoning their own reading experience of more than one text.

The systematic approach to teaching comparison would be as follows.

2h make comparisons within the text

Phase 1	1. **I am learning to recognise similar text types.** This is where pupils explore a variety of formatted extracts and sort them based on what is similar in content and/or appearance. 2. **I am learning to recognise similar themes across texts.** This is where pupils learn to compare texts with similar themes using extracts. 3. **I am learning to identify similar key details across texts.** This is about pupils making comparisons of similar character traits, descriptions or events across more than one text.
Phase 2	4. **I am learning to identify differences in characters' personalities, actions or events.** This is about looking at how the protagonist and the antagonist is established within a text using polar descriptions or looking at differences between characters who may not necessarily be on opposing sides of a narrative. In the case of non-fiction texts, this is about comparing different outcomes of events or different key facts around subjects. 5. **I am learning to compare and contrast across sections of a text.** This is about pupils identifying differences and similarities in detail across one text be it through characters, actions or events.

How to teach reading domains in cognitive sequence

The National Curriculum does not make it apparent in which order the skills of comprehension should be taught. The descriptions of the various domains are broad but by deeply analysing them, there are clear overlaps and links which are often the cause of inconsistencies in teaching methodology. Now that we have unpacked each domain area, what remains is to sequence them in a way that makes sense. There is not only a systematic way to teach each skill to build robustness in visible comprehension but a sequential order to teaching the reading domains which will vastly improve how pupils access and understand texts.

The following pathway has been tried and tested over many years of classroom practice and has proven to be the most impacting pathway of clarity based on the apparent links between domains stated in the curriculum.

The domain sequencing steps (Figure 9) give priority to teaching a child to clarify the meaning of words and phrases (2a). Vocabulary and meaning is paramount and a great deal of time should be spent enabling pupils to become strategists in working out meaning for themselves. It is a skill that must be consistently revisited no matter what domain is being taught as the main focus. The same can be said of retrieval (2b). However, retrieval is often firstly taught as a soft skill prior to explicit teaching, e.g. quick fire recall of simple details such as repetition of names or echoing what was read.

Once pupils are taught strategies for clarifying the meaning of language, they are primed to be taught shades of meaning writers intend for the reader as they can use these skills to help pick up on the nuances of vocabulary chosen. With shades of meaning under their belt, the ability to infer is reinforced with language that reflects the emotive scale of intensity in a text. Without this, their expression of

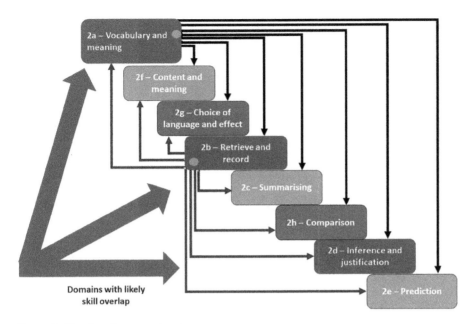

Figure 9: *The domain sequencing steps*

inference will often miss the mark. With the ability to justify, pupils will make more sensible predictions with the knowledge that they will need to support their elaborative inference with text evidence.

It is important that pupils are taught the skill of retrieval prior to summarising. They rely on this skill greatly when it comes to rounding up key details to determine main ideas, following which comparisons can be made. Through summarising, they are able to develop the language of evaluation which will lend itself to sensible reasoning around comparisons within and across texts.

Where a text provides more opportunities for retrieval, it is important that 2b, 2c and 2h stick together in a block of learning as they are complementary. Where a text lends itself towards inferring, 2a, 2f, 2g, 2d and 2e should be taught together as complementary skills and in this order. Retrieval, once taught explicitly, will then overlap with vocabulary and meaning if synonyms are used in questioning instead of exact words or phrases from the text, which makes locating the right response more challenging.

Once Phase 1 is accomplished and pupils are demonstrating more automatic application of the strategies taught, there is no need to necessarily follow this sequenced approach. Overlapping of skills requires reader experience and maximised opportunities to have practiced each in order to recognise what they are being required to demonstrate. At Phase 2, teaching should be pragmatic with a focus on skills to enable pupils to cope with the cognitive demand of full language comprehension. This means that if a text provides the possibility of demonstrating more than one reading skill, then pupils should be adept at doing so. The overlapping of skills is a frequent feature for the testable domains where you often see more than one skill being demanded of the pupils in one question. In order for Phase 2 to be fully understood in pedagogy, the art of questioning needs to be refined.

The following table is a useful skills progression map which demonstrates how the mastery approach breakdown of skills builds up in challenge and depth for KS2. The domains are placed in systematic order to ensure foundation skills are taught which then overlap with skills of higher cognitive demand.

Skills progression map for KS2 Phase 1 and Phase 2

2b	2c	2h	2a
I am learning to link key words to a section of text.	I am learning to retell the key details in a section of a story/non-fiction text.	I am learning to recognise similar key detail.	I am learning to identify unfamiliar vocabulary.
I am learning to identify the key details in a section of a text.	I am learning to retell the whole of a story/non-fiction text using my own words.	I am learning to identify differences in characters' personalities/actions.	I am learning to recognise strategies for clarifying meaning.
I am learning to retrieve key supporting detail.	I am learning to annotate the main ideas of a story/ non-fiction text using my own words.	I am learning to compare and contrast across sections of a text.	I am learning to apply strategies to find meaning.
I am learning to record and present key details from a text (non-fiction).	I am learning to record the correct sequence of a story/non-fiction text.	I am learning to compare and contrast themes across texts.	I am learning to retrieve words for a given meaning.
I am learning to recognise how main ideas are presented in a text (non-fiction).	I am learning to record the main ideas across sections of text using my own words.		I am learning to give words with similar meanings.
I am learning to identify features and their meaning in newspaper reports, poetry, diary entries, etc.).			I am learning to link groups of words to a similar phrase.
I am learning to summarise the main ideas in sections of a text.			I am learning to identify a word closest in meaning.
I am learning to sequence the main ideas of a whole text.			I am learning to explain the meaning of words.
I am learning to record factual details in a text.			I am learning to explain the meanings of phrases.
I am learning to record key details/main ideas of a text.			

2f	2g	2d	2e
I am learning to locate key features given in a text.	I am learning to recognise emotive words in a text.	I am learning to identify an opinion.	I am learning to predict possible outcomes from stated details.
I am learning to annotate key features of a text.	I am learning to identify words that give emotive effect in a text.	I am learning to find evidence for a given opinion.	I am learning to predict possible outcomes from implied details.
I am learning to recognise the purpose of key features of a text.	I am learning to recognise shades of meaning from words in context.	I am learning to give an understanding from given text evidence.	I am learning to justify predictions given.
I am learning to identify the purpose of key features of a text.	I am learning to identify shades of meaning from questions about a text.	I am learning to give an opinion about a character's personality/actions and prove it.	I am learning to fully explain a prediction and justify.
I am learning to discuss themes and conventions of a genre.	I am learning to recognise groups of words that changes the tone of a text.	I am learning to prove/ disprove a given opinion.	
I am learning to identify themes and conventions of a genre.	I am learning to identify when the tone of a text changes.	I am learning to fully explain an opinion and justify it with evidence.	
I am learning to recognise the writer's techniques in a text.	I am learning to explain how language affects the tone of a text.	I am learning to justify varied opinions given.	
I am learning to identify the purpose of the writer's techniques in a text.	I am learning to recognise figurative language in a text.		
I am learning to explain the effect of the writer's techniques in a text.	I am learning to explain how figurative language affects the reader.		

Key for skills progression map

Dark grey objectives are to be taught in Phase 1.

Light grey objectives are to be taught in either Phase 1 or Phase 2 as pupils become more confident.

White objectives are to be taught in Phase 2 with increasing independence.

4 How to use standards to build comprehension questioning

Knowledge of the existing reading test framework (STA, 2015) around questioning is an invaluable thing. Although the frameworks for both KS1 and KS2 exist in order for teachers to be aware of what will be tested for reading comprehension benchmark SATs as well as how the tests are designed, it is an excellent resource for learning how to create questions in everyday teaching in order to guide pupils to demonstrate their comprehension of texts to the right standards. The aim here is to ensure that teachers are aware of the types of cognitive processes pupils should be exposed to when responding to test questions around a text.

The frameworks do not replace what is to be taught in the reading curriculum and must not be considered the totality of what reading comprehension teaching entails, nor are they meant to inform regular statutory teacher assessments for the simple reason that they only deal with the testable domains, which we have already established are linked to many other curriculum areas – though not all. As teacher assessments in reading have been removed since the 2018–2019 cycle (STA, 2018), attainment purely relies on pupils being able to demonstrate their mastery of comprehension through the test results. Whether or not we are in agreement of this is another matter altogether. However, it is certainly the job of teachers to make sure pupils are prepared for standardised questioning whether in test format or not. Therefore we will use the KS2 test framework for its notable value – which is to pull from this the knowledge needed to inform the art of comprehension questioning and response regulation.

Although reading test papers for Year 6 come in the form of three texts, each of increasing difficulty, the following advice is based on the presumption that all pupils are accessing the same quality text within a lesson.

A summary of the cognitive demand of questions

The KS2 test framework (STA, 2015) is based on five strands of cognitive demand, under which questions are sorted according to their level of difficulty. The scale for difficulty is 1 (easiest) to 4 (most difficult). The five areas of cognitive demand are:

1   Strand A – Accessibility of the target information, i.e. 'Where can the information be found?' (p.9)
2   Strand B – Complexity of the target information, i.e. 'What is the language of the text like?' (p.9)
3   Strand C – Task-specific complexity, i.e. 'How much work is needed to answer the question?' (p.9)
4   Strand D – Response strategy, i.e. 'How easy is it to organise and present the answer?' (p.10)
5   Strand E – Technical knowledge required, i.e. 'How complex is the language of the question and/or the knowledge needed to answer it?' (p.10)

Strand A – 'Where can the information be found?'

The location of the information that informs the reader's response determines the cognitive processes for the reader. According to the STA if the information is easily spotted in the text – i.e. in prominent locations, limited to one or two answers, related to a small section of text, has obvious vocabulary links between question and text (same or similar wording) and is obvious with no need to sieve through text to decide the best response – this is a low challenge question which would be rated as 1 on the difficulty scale. However, if the opposite is true then this is ranked on the scale at 4 – a high challenge question. So what does this look like in practice?

Take for example the following extract from the first chapter of *The Secret Garden* by Frances Hodgson Burnett (1911):

> 'When Mary Lennox was sent to Misselthwaite Manor to live with her uncle everybody said she was the most disagreeable-looking child ever seen. It was true, too. She had a little thin face and a little thin body, thin light hair and a sour expression. Her hair was yellow, and her face was yellow because she had been born in India and had always been ill in one way or another. Her father had held a position under the English Government and had always been busy and ill himself, and her mother had been a great beauty who cared only to go to parties and amuse herself with gay people. She had not wanted a little girl at all, and when Mary was born she handed her over to the care of an Ayah, who was made to understand that if she wished to please the Mem Sahib she must keep the child out of sight as much as possible.'

A scale 1 question example could be: 'Where was Mary sent to live?' As you can see, the information is prominently in the first sentence of the paragraph. The question also shares the same language as the text which makes locating the information very easy, i.e. *sent* and *to live* both appear in the text and the question. Only one response would be required which is simply *Misselthwaite Manor*.

A scale 2 question could be: 'How did Mary appear to her uncle?' The language in the question is not directly linked as 'appear' needs to be interpreted but the subject (uncle) is a clear link to the text which is easily located to find the response of *disagreeable-looking*.

A scale 3 question could be: 'Give four examples from the text of what made Mary *disagreeable-looking*.' Straight away the reader is forced to read on from the linked vocabulary, search for more than two examples from a wider area of text and pick through more than four possible answers which are competing evidence. Pupils could easily say her face, body, hair and colour – which could be regarded as vague – or they could say she *had a thin face, little thin body, thin light hair, sour expression and a yellow complexion*. They are clearly given a 'locator' (*disagreeable-looking*) around which information is to be read for a response.

A scale 4 question could be: 'How can you tell that Mary had a difficult childhood?' This certainly ramps up the cognitive demand as the only linking word is the subject 'Mary' and there is much to be said about her in this section. Pupils will need to read a wider section of the text and sieve through the information in which there is some competing evidence. Mary did have a carer (*Mem Sahib*) which some could interpret as being looked after well despite the other evidence which the question demands an analysis of. Mary being persistently ill and not wanted by her mother because she was a girl, as well as the fact that her mother chose not to care for her instead handing her over to the care of *an Ayah* is really the type of answer you would be looking for.

What we can learn from this in the practice of questioning is to think carefully about the number of simple questions we ask and to be aware of how to increase challenge by recognising the cognitive work required to locate information needed to form a response as well as the design of the vocabulary links between questions and texts.

Strand B – 'What is the language of the text like?'

This is more about the level of challenge when it comes to decoding and understanding a text as opposed to the level of challenge in the vocabulary of the questions. This is particularly about how the three texts in a reading test rank from scale 1 to scale 4. At the lowest end of the scale, information needed for answering questions is less abstract with more familiar vocabulary and low 'lexico-grammatical density' (STA, 2015) which simply means there are fewer adjectives, verbs, nouns and adverbs as well as easily read functioning words, i.e. those of purely grammatical purpose which support the meaning-making vocabulary in the text. Many may interpret this as just word count, but the 2019 SATs test showed that word count does not necessarily mean difficulty in readability. Certainly, the third text in the booklet titled *Music Box* was a lengthy text of 903 words. The text was scored as a very easy read when using Flesch reading ease analysis, while *The Park* and *Fact Sheet: About Bumblebees* scored a more standard or average reading ease score despite being shorter texts.

When selecting comprehension texts for the purpose of testing, the Lexile framework (Smith and Turner, 2016) is a somewhat useful tool. Mirroring the length of text extracts in practice helps to ensure pupils maintain stamina. However, it is not the be-all and end-all. In other words, while the framework suggests that in KS2, Year 3 should aim at word counts of up to 1200 (Lexile range of 400–640), Year 4 up to 1400 (Lexile range 620–790), Year 5 up to 1600 (Lexile range 770–870) and Year 6 up to 1700 (Lexile range up 850–980), this does not mean a teacher cannot choose a shorter extract with more challenging language or a slightly longer one with easier vocabulary. What the framework does do is to give us a boundary to ensure we are not under-exposing pupils to lengthier texts and hence deterring the reading stamina necessary both for reading a book in its entirety or for being tested at national standards. Fundamentally, the Lexile range of a text based on the lexico-grammatical density does not determine the level of challenge needed to comprehend it. Hence, the choice of quality text with rich vocabulary and varied use of language and content from wide ranges of genres is more essential than to go plunking in extracts in a Flesch readability calculator every time one is selected. Ensuring that rich texts are taught in reading comprehension allows for pupils to tackle reading skills in high-challenge thresholds.

Strand C – 'How much work is needed to answer the question?'

This is an especially useful tool around the design of questions for everyday teaching practice. This strand focuses on scaling questions based on the level of complexity in cognitive processes required for responding. In other words, where a question does not require pupils to infer or use any of the higher reading skills (such as analysis or evaluation), this would be regarded as a scale 1: low complexity question. This also applies where the task requires pupils to use basic knowledge in order to respond, e.g. simple retrieval questions with close vocabulary links to the text. This ramps up to scale 4 in many ways. Questions can become more challenging when they require multiple responses – for instance, it is less challenging when the same skill is applied to give more than one answer for a question in a simple response zone (e.g. tick two). However, this can become more challenging when the skill is applied within an answer zone that expands to include written responses (e.g. two succinct written answer lines). Questions can also increase in challenge when domains overlap, e.g. a two-part question where the response to one part is simple retrieval and the second response is inference, even where the answer zone is more concrete (such as circle or tick). Likewise, when the question requires a use of inference or the higher cognitive areas and the response zone moves from a one-line written response to a two-part column response with a mix of missing and completed text or to a response zone of several lines for full explanations therefore requiring a fully abstract.

Examples

The following is an example of what could be regarded as a scale 1 question taken from the 2016 KS2 reading SATs paper:

The tiny island, thick with creeping vines and roots, looked as if it floated. At its centre, an ancient oak tree towered over it. The tree's branches were like bent fingers, twisting and stretching outwards, until the tips of its leaves touched the still water. Oliver carefully steered the boat through a narrow opening in the branches. Then

Figure 10: *The Lost Queen, extract from KS2 SATs reading booklet 2016, p.5*

Section 1: The Lost Queen

Qu.	Requirement	Mark
7	Write down **three** things that you are told about the oak tree on the island. **Content domain:** 2b – retrieve and record information / identify key details from fiction and non-fiction	Up to 3m

Figure 11: *The Lost Queen, extract from KS2 SATs mark scheme 2016, p.10*

As you can see, there is a clear vocabulary link between the question and the text – 'oak tree'. The retrieval is simple and only made slightly more challenging by requiring multiple responses.

The following is an example of what could be regarded as a scale 2 question type taken from the 2016 SATs paper:

It was a name.

Maria's family name.

"You could have been a queen?" said Oliver, whispering.

Maria laughed gently in the gloom.

"We were the family of the lion," she said.

Figure 12: *The Lost Queen text extract from 2016 Reading SATS booklet, p.5*

10	What was revealed at the end of the story?	1m
	Tick **one**.	
	Content domain: 2b – retrieve and record information / identify key details from fiction and non-fiction	
	Award 1 mark for:	
	Oliver was keeping a secret. ☐	
	The monument was damaged. ☐	
	The two families were still enemies. ☐	
	Maria's family did not win the throne. ☑	

Figure 13: *The Lost Queen, extract from KS2 SATs mark scheme 2016, p.11*

While this is also a retrieval question, some cognitive work is needed in terms of the interpretation of what the word 'could' implies in the text. The answers presented are not an exact match to the text but subtly test pupils' ability to make grammatical connections to meaning. However, the response zone is quite low on the difficulty scale as pupils only have to tick one of the answers from the options given.

The following are some examples of what could be regarded as a scale 3 question type taken from the 2016 KS2 Reading SATs paper:

Maria led Oliver across the tangled ground to the hidden monument. It was a column of marble, weathered and mossy with age. A delicate crown sat at the top, and an inscription was carved into a flat slab at the base. Oliver used his thumbnail to scrape out the letters that were cut into it.

Figure 14: *The Lost Queen, extract from KS2 SATs reading booklet 2016, p.5*

Section 1: The Lost Queen

Qu.	Requirement	Mark
9a	Look at the paragraph beginning: *Maria led Oliver...*	1m
	Why did Oliver find it difficult to read the inscription on the monument?	
	Content domain: 2d – make inferences from the text / explain and justify inferences with evidence from the text	
9b	What did he have to do in order to read the inscription?	1m
	Content domain: 2b – retrieve and record information / identify key details from fiction and non-fiction	

Figure 15: *The Lost Queen, extract from KS2 SATs mark scheme 2016, p.11*

9 Look at the paragraph beginning: *Maria led Oliver...*

(a) Why did Oliver find it difficult to read the inscription on the monument?

_____
1 mark

(b) What did he have to do in order to read the inscription?

_____
1 mark

Figure 16: *The Lost Queen, extract from KS2 SATs answer booklet 2016, p.6*

As you can see this is a two part question where pupils have to use multiple skills of inference and simple retrieval to demonstrate comprehension. The presence of inference creates more challenge to cognitive demand but the response zone requires a succinct response. The line in the response zone, as well as the score, indicates that there is less abstract thinking required. However, there is a clear connection between the inference question and the vocabulary in the text, narrowing the section where the information needs to be found for a response.

The following is an example of what could be regarded as a scale 4 question type taken from the 2016 KS2 Reading SATs paper:

Section 2: Wild Ride

Qu.	Requirement	Mark
21	In what ways might Martine's character appeal to many readers? Explain fully, referring to the text in your answer. **Content domain:** 2d – make inferences from the text / explain and justify inferences with evidence from the text	Up to 3m

Figure 17: *The Wild Ride, extract from KS2 SATs answer booklet 2016, p.19*

This question requires a very abstract response and there is no direct link between the text and the key focus vocabulary of the question. It demands that readers should, in essence, infer. However, there is an overlapping of skills here as certainly they will need to make mental comparisons in order to evaluate how the character would appeal, therefore needing to sieve out the relevant text to prove each point and disregard any competing evidence which does not.

The knowledge of how questions are developed within the SATs papers is very useful when creating quality questions for comprehension that will stretch and challenge for depth of skill application.

Strand D – 'How easy is it to organise and present the answer?'

It is also important for teachers to consider the zone of response. The response zone is normally manipulated in a KS2 test according how much work it takes to gather information and present an answer. The lowest rating of scale 1 is usually those response zones where the answers are very brief and there is a direct indication of the structure of the response in either the question or in the response zone. For example, where it says circle or tick with options given, this would be a low challenge response zone – although this does not imply the question is an easy one! The difficulty again scales up to 4 where the response zone requires a fully developed answer with lengthier writing using the reader's own vocabulary and structure.

This strand helps teachers to design or choose questions where the response zone is varied. Some of the response zones offer some amount of scaffolding which will prompt meaning-making from less confident readers before moving them on to more independent structures. Bearing in mind that pupils who struggle to write will generally struggle to demonstrate their comprehension in a fully developed answer, other types of response zones still gives them the ability to show they do understand the text and may simply need to be taught how to structure fully developed responses.

The following are examples of what could be regarded as a scale 1 response zone from the 2018 KS2 Reading SATs answer booklet:

7 Look at the section headed: **Other interesting facts**.

Complete the sentence below.

Recent studies show that…

Tick **one**.

giant pandas always spend most of their lives alone.	☐
most giant pandas live in captivity.	☐
giant pandas only live in the wild in China.	☐
some giant pandas live in the same area.	☐ 1 mark

Figure 18: *The Giant Panda Bear, extract from KS2 SATs answer booklet 2018, p.6*

The possible answers are all present in the response zone, there is a clear indication of how many will be required to solve and the given statements are succinct.

8 Look at the section headed: **Why are people concerned about the giant panda?**

Find and **copy one** word which shows that there are lots of things we do not yet know about giant pandas.

_____   1 mark

Figure 19: *The Giant Panda Bear, extract from KS2 SATs answer booklet 2018, p.7*

This question also clearly indicates the type of response required with a short line as a clue that only one word is required as an answer.

The following is an example of what could be regarded as a scale 2 response zone from the 2018 KS2 Reading SATs answer booklet:

10 According to the text, why are giant pandas under threat of extinction?

Give **two** reasons.

1. _____

2. _____   2 marks

Figure 20: *The Giant Panda Bear, extract from KS2 SATs answer booklet 2018, p.8*

Although this question does also indicate how many answers are required and the answer zone is deliberately in a list of two points to be completed, the challenge is simply that it moves from one or two word answers to full statements of reasoning.

The following are examples of what could be regarded as scale 3 response zones from the 2018 KS2 Reading SATs answer booklet:

24 *She hobbled through the ward to where I lay*
And drew quite close and, hesitating, peered.

Why does she hesitate?

_____
                                                    1 mark

Figure 21: *Grannie, extract from KS2 SATs answer booklet 2018, p.13*

In this instance, there is no indicator of how many responses are required. The layout of the response zone suggests a succinct answer that is longer than just one word.

38 Look at page 10.

What impressions do you get of Em Sharp at this point in the extract?

Give **two** impressions, using evidence from the text to support your answer.

Impression	Evidence

                                                    3 marks

Figure 22: *Albion's Dream, extract from KS2 SATs answer booklet 2018, p.20*

Although this question type may appear tricky, it clearly has an indication of how many responses are necessary and is partly structured in the booklet for the pupils to simply fill in the answers. What may have been more challenging are the facts that the impression response zone is indicated by a short line in each which implies very succinct answers and that the evidence has three lines. Pupils will have to structure their answers within these response zones so some thought will have to be given to this.

The following is an example of what could be regarded as a scale 4 response zone from the 2017 KS2 Reading SATs answer booklet:

33 Look at page 9.

How is the whale made to seem mysterious?

Explain **two** ways, giving evidence from the text to support your answer.

_____

_____

_____

_____

_____

_____

_____   3 marks

Figure 23: *An Encounter at Sea, extract from KS2 SATs answer booklet 2017, p.16*

This type of question does not have a clear indication of structure. Even though it specifies the number of explanations to be included in the response, it does not state the number of pieces of evidence needed to support. The layout suggests fully developed answers are required from the pupils which they will need to structure on their own to ensure there is a flow between their own inference and their justification. This is quite a challenging lengthier response for most pupils and although such a question type has not appeared since the 2017 KS2 reading test, this does not mean it may never appear in the future.

Strand E – 'How complex is the language of the question and/or the knowledge needed to answer it?'

A question ranked on scale 1 would be one with highly accessible and uncomplicated vocabulary containing no 'subject-specific technical language' (STA, 2015). It is important to note that the technical vocabulary referred to in this strand are those words whose meanings are not present in the text. This goes up to scale 4 where the language becomes very complex in meaning and subject-specific vocabulary not found in the text is present. This is very much about the reader's knowledge of vocabulary and meaning both in terms of the question and the text itself. Strand E helps teachers to look into how questions are being designed, useful for differentiating questioning style without minimising the cognitive challenge necessary to answer. Start by considering whether the language of the question is easily understood or loaded with technical or complex language. Certainly, uncomplicated language does not mean a higher order cognitive skill isn't required to answer the question.

The following is an example of what could be regarded as a scale 1 knowledge-based question from the 2017 KS2 Reading SATs answer booklet:

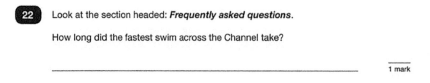

22 Look at the section headed: *Frequently asked questions.*

How long did the fastest swim across the Channel take?

_____   ‾‾‾‾
1 mark

Figure 24: *An Encounter at Sea, extract from KS2 SATs answer booklet 2017, p.11*

The vocabulary here is easy to interpret, with the same vocabulary present in the text itself. Pupils would easily know what the Channel is by its use in the text.

The following is an example of what could be regarded as a scale 2 knowledge-based question, also from the 2017 KS2 SATs answer booklet:

15 *Nearly twenty-two hours later, the exhausted man staggered onto French soil at Calais and became an instant hero.*

Find and **copy two** different words from the sentence above that show how tired Matthew Webb was.

1. _____

2. _____   ‾‾‾‾
1 mark

Figure 25: *Swimming the English Channel, extract from KS2 SATs answer booklet 2017, p.9*

Although the word 'tired' is easily understood by the reader, there is added challenge in terms of the evidence in the text. Pupils would have to recognise that 'exhausted' is a state of being 'very tired' and that 'staggered' suggests weakness from being very tired. While the question itself is easily understood, the extract given from the text as the location of the answer involves some knowledge of what the language choice implies.

Figure 26 shows an example of what could be regarded as a scale 3 knowledge-based question from the 2017 KS2 Reading SATs mark scheme. This question is of similar design. The level of challenge comes from both the choices of answers as well as the knowledge required to link to the text evidence. Pupils would have to know that 'putt-putt' tells the reader the boat was making intermittent noises, i.e. chugging. The difficulty here is they would also have to eliminate the other choices based on their knowledge of what these things would look like or sound like. Without a background knowledge of these answers, pupils would struggle to identify 'chugging' as the correct answer. It is likely that many would pick up on the word 'engine' and link to 'racing' or 'roaring', ignoring the rest of the quote which also holds key meaning for interpreting 'putt-putt'. Providing they had interpreted the first response accurately, they would then have to have a mental image that mirrors 'stillness', which would eliminate 'bubbling ripples' and 'rocking tide'. There is also no connection between the choice 'cold sea' and the evidence provided.

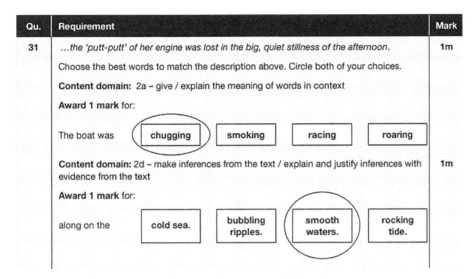

Qu.	Requirement	Mark
31	*...the 'putt-putt' of her engine was lost in the big, quiet stillness of the afternoon.*	1m
	Choose the best words to match the description above. Circle both of your choices.	
	Content domain: 2a – give / explain the meaning of words in context	
	Award 1 mark for:	
	The boat was · (chugging) · smoking · racing · roaring	
	Content domain: 2d – make inferences from the text / explain and justify inferences with evidence from the text	1m
	Award 1 mark for:	
	along on the · cold sea. · bubbling ripples. · (smooth waters.) · rocking tide.	

Figure 26: *An Encounter at Sea KS2 mark scheme extract (2017), p.20*

Figure 27 shows an example of what could be regarded as a scale 4 knowledge-based question from the KS2 2017 Reading SATS mark scheme. There are several examples of subject-specific vocabulary in this question, the meaning of which cannot be located in the text. Pupils would have to know what *section* and *main content* means. Within the answer choices, the language is complex with further

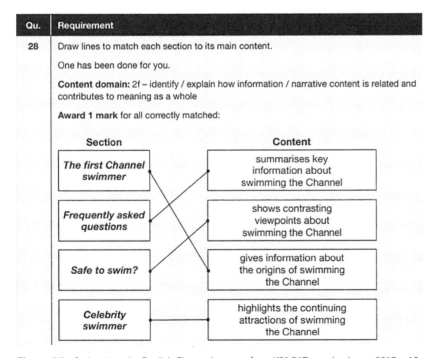

Qu.	Requirement
28	Draw lines to match each section to its main content.
	One has been done for you.
	Content domain: 2f – identify / explain how information / narrative content is related and contributes to meaning as a whole
	Award 1 mark for all correctly matched:

Figure 27: *Swimming the English Channel, extract from KS2 SATs mark scheme 2017, p.18*

technical references within the content descriptors. Words like *summarises, contrasting, viewpoints, origins* are all technical and are dependent on the reader's own knowledge of what this means.

By using the above methods as a part of question design, teachers can be very targeted in test preparation. In the everyday classroom, use of the rigorously researched methods employed by the STA will ensure questioning of text is purposeful and standards are linked in a way that makes for resilient pupils in test conditions.

5 Questioning techniques that build comprehension mastery

Questioning is the teaching tool that opens up a child's ability to make their comprehension visible. It is not for the purpose of testing only – in fact, testing is last on the list of things it is best suited for. As a part of a teacher's toolkit, questioning acts as an enabler for rich discussion and knowledge exchange. When teaching for mastery, the ability to use questioning effectively is based on sound differentiation and assessment.

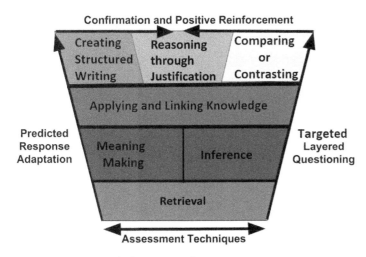

Figure 28: *Framework of questioning for mastery*

What usually poses as a challenge for us as teachers is whether we are questioning enough or whether we are using challenging questions. However, what needs to be certain is that cognitive overload does not occur. The only way for this to be avoided is to ensure pupils develop their ability to probe text in a structured and systematic manner. The Bloom's taxonomy approach is the most proven methodology of questioning that encourages increased cognitive ability. The framework diagram (see Figure 28) is an adaptation of Bloom's pyramid based on developing probing readers for mastery. The outside arrows are the principles of pedagogy that inform the art of questioning for mastery.

Underpinning everything is persistent assessment – from formative to summative, of which formative is of the utmost importance every lesson. Teachers need to be persistently mapping misconceptions in order to question effectively. Misconception mapping is about noticing where pupils make errors in understanding as much as predicting where errors may occur in comprehension. Once misconceptions become more predictive, teachers need to have the ability to adapt their questioning in order to avoid simply giving pupils the answer. In other words – if a child errs in thinking, what strategies will the teacher readily provide that will guide them to the correct understanding and empower them to self-correct? There is also the fact that questioning needs to be targeted and layered for the use of particular skills in order to match the appropriate strategies necessary for these skills to result in visible comprehension. Questions also have to be designed on a system of ramping up – in order to increase challenge and work the cognitive muscle – while pupils practice strategies in different contexts.

Finally, there needs to be both confirmation and positive reinforcement. Confirmation means teachers must tell pupils when they are correct and when they are not. Too often, teachers mollycoddle pupils when errors are made. This is highly unnecessary and in fact denies pupils the ability to develop a growth mindset. It is for this reason many pupils crumble when they make a mistake rather than try again. Pupils not only need boundaries, but absolutely appreciate them, especially when working towards mastery. When they make a mistake, if they don't know why it isn't correct, they often simply disregard the negative feeling it brings and move on – that is a learning opportunity lost. It is therefore quite important that feedback is immediately given and is constructive. One of the problems with marking answers to comprehension questions the day after is that the child has long forgotten the text and when revisiting it, it will take them some time to edit and improve answers. For this reason, I never recommend marking outside of lessons – to be honest, I never recommend marking unless it is for the purpose of simply annotating 'verbal feedback given' until pupils are ready to be assessed, but that is a whole other matter altogether. Pupils need to see their misconceptions or refresh their strategy application and make immediate improvements. Collaborative marking of answers in comprehension sessions is a powerful tool and for this reason there should be more practising and whole-class discussions around understanding rather than quizzing and marking after the horse has left the stables so to speak. The trick is to make erroneous responses an integral part of learning. Treat errors as a time for you to teach as opposed to a time for the pupils with the right answers to shine and *thank* them for sharing these misconceptions. Of course, this has to be the ethos of the entire learning atmosphere because from mistakes come learning and growth. Without errors you and I would be rendered irrelevant. Positive reinforcement is simply taking a positive spin on misconceptions and reinforcing the strategy needed to fix them to give pupils the chance to go back to the drawing board and improve their work as quickly as possible after feedback. We do it so often in maths – I argue it is a must in reading comprehension also.

It is often normal practice for teachers to present pupils with a full extract and to develop several questions that challenge pupils to look at the text in a mostly continuous fashion in order to demonstrate several skills at once. This is perfectly fine for the purpose of assessment and when practicing SATs-style papers in preparation for the benchmark exam. However, when teaching for mastery the aim is for pupils to notice every detail in order to have a full understanding through plenty of practice of one skill at a time, until confident in order to then interlink skills organically. This is about developing pupils into probing readers with the ability to investigate beneath and between layers of language in order to see the full picture being painted by a writer. Teachers act as the enabler of confident 'comprehenders' through their ability to generate skill-related questions, predict responses and potential misconceptions, and have a robust knowledge of strategies to support pupils. As pupils grow in confidence, their ability to apply strategies to demonstrate a particular skill must be met with varying degrees of cognitive demand which stretch and challenge their comprehension to greater depth as opposed to breadth.

Question type recognition strategies

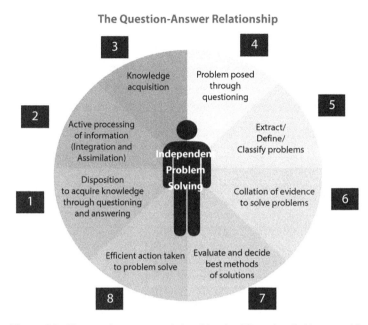

The Question-Answer Relationship

Figure 29: *The question-answer relationship wheel (based on Robinson and Rackstraw, 1975)*

The relationship between questioning and answering is intrinsic to comprehension confidence. The inability to recognise question types often leads to the incorrect cognitive demand being applied, e.g. not recognising a question involves multiple skills or a movement from concrete responses to abstract ones. Sensitising pupils to the type of question they see and hear empowers them to pull on the most appropriate comprehension strategies with confidence and give more accurate responses. The question-answer relationship model (see Figure 29) is based on the knowledge that pupils are naturally curious about their environment and that they have the desire to acquire knowledge (Robinson and Rackstraw, 1975).

Questioning is more natural than reading itself. Read that again. When we are born, we view all things with curiosity and every sense opens up to the newness of the world. Babies touch and push everything into their mouths as they try to discover what is edible for survival or what will comfort them. The **disposition to acquire knowledge** remains with us for most – if not all – of our lives. If we as teachers always bear this in mind, we would see questioning as a well-needed step towards understanding rather than a well-needed step in testing alone. Questioning is indeed an organic feature of reading teaching. Once we question we seek answers, **actively integrating and assimilating information** while simultaneously compartmentalising detail into short-, working- and long-term memory. Having acquired the knowledge we need, we are armed to tackle **problems posed**. Questioning enables independent problem solving and the key step often missed in the process of building a relationship between questions and answers is modelling how to **extract, define and classify the problems** we are faced with. In other words, if pupils are to answer questions correctly, they first need to be able to analyse the questions. Once they are able to do so effectively, their focus can switch to structuring the appropriate response through **collating the evidence** needed to problem solve. It then becomes about **evaluating and deciding** the best method for solving, i.e. do they write a short answer, long answer, circle, tick, match? Once this is deciphered, pupils can then take **efficient action** to solve the problem. As KS2 teachers, we must model each and every step of the question-answer relationship wheel above. By modelling this, we develop confident and independent problem solvers – that is, pupils are prepared to visibly demonstrate comprehension.

Response structure teaching is and always will be secondary to question structure teaching. Show pupils what you want to see based on them knowing what you have asked – and be systematic about it.

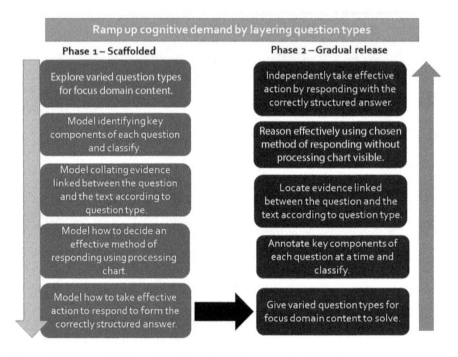

Figure 30: *The question Phase 1 and Phase 2 ramping up methodology chart*

There are two phases of this process. Phase 1 has heavy-to-medium teacher input where you are scaffolding, making use of the process chart (see Figure 46) and doing several models of various question types. In Phase 2, you should move towards release and then independent problem solving.

Firstly, model how to effectively extract and classify the various types of questions pupils can get for focus domain content being taught. This is about 'what does this question demand that I do as a visible comprehender?' as opposed to 'what does this question mean?' Vocabulary and meaning need to be tackled prior to this step. Generally, most comprehension questions fall in the following subsets, inspired by the Question-Answer Relationship (QAR) framework (Raphael and Au, 2005) and shown in Figure 65.

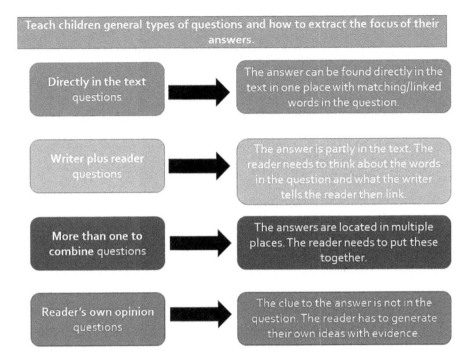

Figure 31: *Question and response relationship chart*

'Directly in the text questions' are those where the structure and vocabulary of the question closely matches the text, e.g. first question, first paragraph with exact words or clear synonyms between the question and the text.

'Writer plus reader questions' means that pupils have to find part of the answer in the text but will have to think about the meaning behind the vocabulary of the text or the vocabulary in the question in order to derive a response. In other words, synonym phrases are used in the question for the vocabulary in the text so there is not a straightforward link between the two.

'More than one to combine' are questions where more than one skill is required in order to problem solve. For example, a question may be asking pupils to retrieve detail, summarise and sequence and they need to be aware of all the skills required of them.

'Reader's own opinion questions' are those where the answer is not directly in the text. Pupils have to use their inference and deduction skills to problem solve.

This awareness of the question and response relationship also builds metacognitive abilities in comprehension as it gives clarity on what is required of the reader. Once taught, pupils can then focus on how to structure their responses in a manner that is fit for purpose.

Another key element of building the question-response relationship is exposing pupils to the varied answer zones. Make them explicitly aware of the cognitive demand of the answer zone by drawing attention to how these areas are visually presented, e.g. short lines, multiple lines, secondary instructions such as tick one, circle or match. Also, when preparing pupils for assessments, sensitise them to the weightings (marks) as they are often a clue to how much cognitive demand is attached to the question being asked.

The teacher as the model of probing reading

When reading aloud to pupils, this is not the time to question. Pupils need the opportunity to hear a text in its entirety and form full perceptions (be they faulty or not), only aided by the intonations and clarity of your modelled reading voice. The worst method of using questioning is to stop mid-read in order to ask a question about a word or an understanding to a child who had already begun to suspend their reality and envision language, only to be brought abruptly out to be quizzed. This is neither helpful nor does it do either of you any good. Reading aloud is your time to bring forward the beauty of a text. The first read-aloud should always be full on, expressive and without interruption. The class environment must be attentive and silent and your voice should command the attention of the room. It is on the second approach to the text that the probing reader begins their quest. The re-read for the purpose of probing should be done in chunks – sentence by sentence or paragraph by paragraph.

At each pausing moment, invoke enquiry by questioning aloud then reasoning aloud. Thinking aloud as a reader makes good comprehension skills visible, thus revealing to pupils how questions naturally arise in the reader's mind while reading. It is also key to demonstrating working through how to actually find answers to such questions derived from the text. Making the inside outside is a pedagogical skill in itself and is the primary technique used when questioning for mastery. It models for pupils the standard of good probing questions that truly explore meaning and will feed into their ability to monitor their own comprehension in the longer run. It is about pupils becoming comfortable investigating the unknown while empowering them with strategies to work through to successful knowledge building.

Differentiation through questioning

Questioning for mastery is reliant on the ability to differentiate using **a targeted layered approach** – first verbally in book talk-ability, before moving to written questions and responses to demonstrate comprehension. This is book talk combined with the ability of pupils to show they understand at various levels as opposed to pleasurable exploration only.

The layered approach to questioning acts as either scaffold, guide or straightforward test purpose enquiry. **Scaffolded questioning** is about moving through the Bloom's taxonomy scale systematically from the easiest cognitive skill to the hardest, according to the ability of the class. **Guided questioning** occurs where there are misconceptions; these questions are designed to help pupils take steps backwards, unpick elements of the text then adapt their responses along the correct lines of thinking in order for them to arrive at the correct understanding. **Test purpose enquiry** mainly happens when pupils are at the advanced stage of comprehension learning and they have been taught and have practised strategies several times with exposure to a wide ranges of texts. These pupils are therefore ready for termly assessments or the benchmark test. Of course, it is also common practice to use **test purpose enquiry** as a baseline at the start of a year to determine what gaps are to be addressed in the autumn term and this can prove to be extremely useful. While there is value in this type of questioning, it is not a teaching tool and therefore should not feature in main lessons unless used for assessment purposes. **Test purpose enquiry** is not a method to achieve mastery.

Scaffolded questioning is really about differentiation across the two phases of teaching: the introduction of skill (Phase 1) and the gradual release to apply skill independently (Phase 2). In the introductory phase of teaching a reading skill, it is important that teachers scaffold questions in a way that allows pupils to:

1   understand the context of the text (the when, what, who, where)

2   understand the meaning of the text (the why)

3   make connections within the text and from text to reader – (the how).

This broad approach provides for rigour in textual analysis which is the ultimate aim, where mastery is demonstrated through the ability to justify or reason and to critically compare and contrast, and the readers' own understanding is coming through when demonstrating their mastery of each skill required across the domains involved. The scaffold within the scaffold comes from looking closely at each step required for the skill to be achieved.

When choosing a text, teachers must first look at the cognitive processes necessary for pupils to understand it before deciding which skill needs to be taught first. If a text lends itself to many inferences, then ensure there is a foundation of skills for inference and justification. It is no use asking pupils to read between the lines when their ability to decipher shades of meaning in vocabulary is weak. Likewise, if pupils cannot even retrieve then perhaps it is best to select a text that lends itself to maximising this skill practice first and so on. Once the order of skills to be taught is linked to text types and decided systematically, for each lesson we must think about how to build in rigorous development of the skill by stretching and challenging its application. As such, questions are to be designed within each session to do just this by using the **ramping up model**:

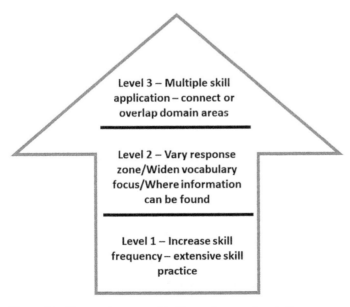

Figure 32: *The ramping up model of increasing question challenge*

The model simply looks at three levels of cognitive demand for each domain area. When questioning, Level 1 is the first point of challenge and is always about questioning in a manner which increases the opportunities to demonstrate the skill. For example, when asking a child to retrieve information from one section, this can be ramped up by asking for more than one piece of information from the same section or from multiple sections.

Here is a standardised example from the 2019 KS2 SATs reading test of how this could be done:

Things you can do to help
Bumblebees help pollinate plants in more than one million acres of British gardens and the flowers they find can be a lifeline for them. No matter how small your garden, you can help to save the sound of summer by providing lots of bee-friendly flowers throughout the year. By 'bee-friendly' we mean flowers that are rich in pollen and nectar. Many ornamental plants that are commonly found in British gardens, such as pansies and begonias, are of no value to wildlife. These decorative and colourful flowers often produce little pollen or nectar. However, there are hundreds of beautiful flowers that do offer these rewards, including foxgloves, lavender, geraniums, herbs and wild roses that you can add to your garden.

Figure 33: *Fact Sheet: About Bumblebees, extract from KS2 SATs reading booklet 2019, p.7.*

Qu.	Requirement	Mark
22 (a)	Look at page 7. Tick one box in each row to show whether each of the following flowers is **bee-friendly** or **not bee-friendly**. **Content domain:** 2b – retrieve and record information / identify key details from fiction and non-fiction **Award 1 mark** for all **four** correct:	1m

	Bee-friendly	Not bee-friendly
lavender	✓	
pansy		✓
herbs	✓	
wild rose	✓	

Figure 34: *Fact Sheet: About Bumblebees, extract from KS2 SATs mark scheme 2019, p.17.*

The above is the extract where the information can be located to answer the question below it. Here, the skill of retrieval needs to be applied multiple times. This gives pupils the opportunity to practise the skill of retrieval while increasing the cognitive demand, as the location of each piece of information is different. Level 2 is about varying how the responses to questions are presented; varying the vocabulary used within the question so that pupils will need to clarify the vocabulary in the question in order to link to the text; or increasing the area where the information needed to respond can be found. For example, instead of simply requiring one word or a list of words in the response zone, include ticking or circling answers or writing short statements. Here is a standardised example using retrieval in part two of the above question:

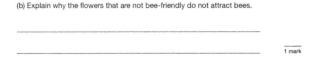

(b) Explain why the flowers that are not bee-friendly do not attract bees.

_____

_____ 1 mark

Figure 35: *Fact Sheet: About Bumblebees, extract from KS2 SATs answer booklet 2019, p.17.*

Notice this is no longer a tick as positive indication but now an explanation which can be lifted from the text. The answer zone now presents itself as two lines. Although related to the same section, the language in the text and the question is no longer closely matched (with the exception of 'bee-friendly' which acts as a **locator** for pupils to refer to the correct part of the text). They now have to also clarify the phrase 'do not attract', which is not evident in the text, and seek the information that will explain this.

Level 3 is about creating a question which challenges more than one reading skill in a two-part question or a single question which requires more than one skill to be used hence overlapping cognitive processes. In the following sample question, you can see there are two domain areas involved, inference and retrieval.

Section 1: The Lost Queen

Qu.	Requirement	Mark

9a	Look at the paragraph beginning: *Maria led Oliver...*
	
	Why did Oliver find it difficult to read the inscription on the monument?
	
	Content domain: 2d – make inferences from the text / explain and justify inferences with evidence from the text
	
	Award 1 mark for reference to any of the following:
	
	   1. it is mossy / dirty
	   2. it is covered
	   3. it is weathered.
	
	Do not accept reference to it being old.
		1m

9b	What did he have to do in order to read the inscription?
	
	Content domain: 2b – retrieve and record information / identify key details from fiction and non-fiction
	
	Award 1 mark for references to scraping out the letters / the moss, e.g.
	
	   • *he scrapes out the stuff in the letters*
	   • *use his thumbnail to scratch the letters out.*
		1m

Figure 36: *The Lost Queen, extract from KS2 SATs mark scheme 2016, p.17*

As this is quite a demanding type of two-part question, ideally it should relate to the same section of text to reduce cognitive load.

Ramping up map for cognitive domains

2a	2b	2c	2d	2e	2f	2g	2h
3 Include add-on skill	3 Overlap summary/ sequence skill	3 Vary response layout	3 Include add-on skill	3 Present contrasting outcomes for justification	3 Move from whole text stylistic to word and symbols	3 Add-on inference skill	3 Compare across themes / text features
2 Move from word to group of words	2 Use synonyms for details in the text	2 Move from summarising features to statements	2 Remove text evidence	2 Move from that which is stated to that which is implied	2 Present varied text layout per genre	2 Link to Vocabulary and meaning	2 Move between comparing and contrasting
1 Increase response frequency	1 Increase response frequency	1 Increase response frequency	1 Increase response frequency	1 Increase response frequency	1 Increase response frequency	1 Increase response frequency	1 Increase response frequency

Figure 37: *Map for increased cognitive demand through question design for KS2 cognitive domains*

Guided questioning

Guided questioning can be used as an immediate response to a misconception. Erroneous answers are often a result of misinterpretation of vocabulary or pupils not applying the correct strategies. While it is tempting to simply give a correction and move on in the essence of time, slowing down the pace in order to really make cognitive processes clearer benefits the whole class. 'Never let a misconception go unnoticed' is a rule for teaching reading comprehension for mastery. When, through discussion, pupils see how to correct an error, others will gain an insight into what to avoid as well as a positive reinforcement of strategy application to increase their understanding of the text.

Guided questioning lesson script exemplar

The following is a lesson delivered in Year 3 based on the text *Charlie and the Chocolate Factory* by Roald Dahl (1995).

Context: The focus of the lesson was to learn to infer and began with the skill of retrieving the best evidence to prove an understanding.

Format: The teacher read aloud page one of Chapter 5 of the text and split this into three paragraphs. For each paragraph, she gave an understanding based on the character Mr. Wonka and asked the pupils to find the evidence which proved her understanding to be correct. For the third paragraph, guided questions were used for a particularly challenging question.

Teacher: Take a look at the paragraph in the yellow box. It is my opinion that Mr. Wonka felt he was more important than the ordinary person, in other words he was quite full of himself. Can you find me one piece of evidence from the text that proves this to be true? [Pauses and gives pupils time to scan and chooses pupils who volunteer answers.]

Child A: Because he always wanted to do his own thing, his way.

Teacher: Interesting thought. However, I asked for evidence from the text. Can you find those words 'he wanted to do things his way' in the text? [Child shakes head]. OK, so remember the question asked for evidence, so what do you have to do? (Here the teacher asserts the strategy retrieval previously taught as find and copy through guided questioning.)

Child B: You need to copy the words from the text and use this as evidence.

Teacher: Correct. (Confirmation given.) And that means this time we do not use our own words because I am looking for specific evidence to prove that Mr. Wonka is full of himself. (Teacher gives boundaries and further clarification of instruction.) So can anyone else help Child A to find the best evidence for this opinion? (Collaborative method used for positive reinforcement. Calling on peers for support removes the negative effect of making a mistake and re-directs the error as a learning point.)

Child C: He is full of himself because it says he brought five pupils to see his factory.

Teacher: Let us think about that evidence and see if it fits with the question. (Teacher asserts the strategy of linking background knowledge to a familiar situation for self-checking.) If I brought five friends to my party does that mean I think I am more important than everyone else? [Child shakes head indicating a negative.] Or does that mean that I am being kind and friendly? [Child nods indicating a positive.] So is there anything else there that would be better evidence?

Child D: Where it says 'shown around personally by me'.

Teacher: [Nods in approval in subtle confirmation.] And if you were to identify the specific word in that phrase that gives the impression of him being full of himself, which word would it be? (Here the teacher challenges for mastery – stretching the cognitive process into demonstrating a specific shade of meaning given in the vocabulary. This is her way of ensuring the whole class also learns to justify their responses.)

Child D: 'Personally'.

Teacher: Correct and indeed him saying 'personally' means that he believes he is very important and that the pupils should feel quite proud to have him and he also adds 'by me'. He could have just said 'shown around by me' instead. (Here the teacher develops further reasoning showing how the language pattern creates meaning therefore increasing retention of the skill.)

Guided questioning brings pupils back to the source, prompts re-thinking and, in a whole-class setting, creates a talk atmosphere that generates collaborative learning. It is a very deliberate process which takes into account the smaller cognitive steps, clarifies misconceptions with a balance of examples and thought provocation – all without giving the answer away. Each error is unravelled for the benefit of all.

Questioning for monitoring comprehension using book talk-ability

Book talk-ability is the most powerful way to develop mastery in reading comprehension. The more pupils talk about the texts they read, the more they understand; reading rich books leads to a deeper understanding as knowledge unfolds. Pupils then develop the confidence to verbalise their inquisitiveness. Questioning in this context feels organic and natural and should feature as a part of every lesson with a fairly loose structure. Notably, this is not the same as book talk for pleasure as the role of the teacher during book talk-ability is to persistently model and positively reinforce strategies that will lead to answers to the questions pupils present. The cognitive pressure is removed during book talk-ability as it is the teacher who is open to respond with no expectations for the pupils to follow through to find answers. It is that moment when pupils feel safe to question the teacher and each other that we become most aware of how text affects reasoning. While creating practice questions on paper and sticking them in books as 'evidence' is often what is expected, reading comprehension books should be a collage of how each child becomes a probing reader and the evidence we truly need to see is how they reason through a text to achieve full understanding. The teacher's voice should always be secondary to the reader's voice in truly rich evidence. Reading journals including this element of reflective questioning of the inner reading child are the best ones. In order for pupils to develop self-awareness, they need the space to verbally express what they do or do not understand.

During whole-class reading sessions, book talk-ability occurs after reading aloud a section of text and is always done in the context of a book – not an extract (where reasoning aloud is usually attached to a learning intention). Teaching from books is common practice, therefore there is always room for book talk-ability which aids the comprehension process. After reading aloud, re-reading independently gives pupils the opportunity to participate. Invite pupils to question by first opening up with a question yourself to create collaboration through verbal reasoning. Your tone should be conversational and this gives the pupils the opportunity to relax into their natural discourse. Here is an example of book talk-ability questioning after reading a few pages from the book *Blackberry Blue* by Jamila Gavin (2014) to Year 6.

Book talk-ability questioning lesson script

Teacher: Wow – wasn't that an interesting part of the chapter? There was a bit that really grabbed my attention. Let's re-read this paragraph and tell me what you think about it. [Places section under the visualiser and re-reads.] What do you think about how the people on the bus reacted?

Child A: [interjecting] Yeah! And they held their heads down – what's that about?

Child B: It's because they were scared of that lady.

Teacher: Yes, it looks so because it says here this one was covering their face and another was grabbing their basket and most of them looked down (teacher models retrieving evidence to prove the opinion given). I wouldn't like to be on this journey, would you?

Child C: Just imagine though how could she just be kidnapping pupils and nobody locks her up. I don't get it…

Child B: But they can't lock her up. Can't you see it's magical? I mean someone can't just appear on the other side of the rails and she is normal. How can she do that if she is normal?

Child D: I think she's a witch.

Teacher: Hmmm… interesting idea. Let's see… I wonder if I can find the section that implies she might be a witch…

Child B: Yes – where it says … [reads section from the text]. I don't get what that means though? What does it mean by … [quotes from the section read]?

Teacher: Oh well, this word means hidden and we all know what a hoodie looks like – you wear them all the time – but it looks like her hood was quite large. Think about costumes or characters who wear a hood… (Teacher activates prior knowledge and makes use of intertextual links.)

Child C: Oh like Red Riding Hood. She wears a large hood.

Teacher: Yes – like that but this time it is purple and so large her face is hidden inside. I like when the author uses the phrase… [quotes from a further on section in order to move the discussion along]. It makes her hounds sound sinister as in very scary like they could attack anyone. They don't even sound like normal dogs…

Child E: [interjecting] They sound predatory! Like wolves!

Teacher: I like that word – predatory. The movement of them as the book says here [reads quote] definitely sounds predatory. The vocabulary here is full of imagery used to give the reader impressions in their head. We are going to learn how to clarify figurative language today using our inference and discuss how it makes the reader feel. (Teacher then rounds up the book talk-ability element and focuses on the learning intention by linking their discussion to the skill they are about to explore.)

The flow of this discussion was a thing of magic with even readers developing in confidence actively participating. Straight away you are able to see that particular pupils demonstrated good background knowledge that would assist them and their peers with understanding the text. You can also tell which pupils struggled with the tone of the text and which are already showing signs of monitoring their own comprehension. In the final moments of this session, the teacher allowed pupils to read ahead and jot down any questions they had on sticky notes and place them in their journals for the following lesson. Despite this being a less formal discussion, the teacher capitalised on opportunities to model good text use and gave the pupils space to explore, sound their opinions and their 'wow moments' while at the same time being a facilitator for collaborative learning. The more knowledgeable pupils acted as teachers for their peers when they had valid input to bring to the discussion. If the information wasn't correct or if it sparked their own curiosity, they felt free to interject in order to add-on or clarify. Notably, there were no hands up and the teacher remained seated for this part of the lesson, only standing when re-routing to the focus of the learning.

Book talk-ability sessions should feature within two out of five sessions for the week at least, in order for pupils to develop questioning through verbal reasoning and builds their metacognitive awareness of their own understanding as readers. Afterwards, it is acceptable to shift the method of questioning to the practice of reasoning and wondering aloud led by the teacher making the inside outside and focusing on strategies taught.

Making the inside outside

Reasoning and wondering aloud is the teacher truly modelling the comprehension process. But what does this look like in practice? The aim of making the inside outside is to verbalise the multifaceted cognitive processes behind understanding text. There are systematic steps which underpin thinking aloud and can be applied to any text. These are:

- questioning for clarification
- investigative text scanning
- recall and sorting of relevant strategies to enable comprehension

- application of strategies and deliberate repair of misconceptions in order to analyse text
- positive clarification of understanding in response to original question posed.

Overall this is the core process but there are some variations depending on whether or not pupils participate in the process.

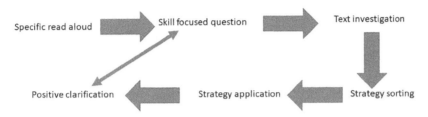

Figure 38: *Core process for reasoning and wondering aloud*

Reasoning and wondering aloud is very much a part of strategy teaching where the teacher first models how strategies are applied through the eyes of a skilled reader. It shows which strategy is fit for purpose and when to apply it during the reading of a text when focussed on a particular cognitive area. It also provides an opportunity to show pupils how to use strategies as a tool – making them the master of the strategy rather than the strategy being their master so to speak. You get the opportunity to show how to tweak, adapt and repeat strategies until the correct understanding is achieved, hence teaching your young readers how to be resilient and unafraid of first failed attempts as well as how to use strategies to their personal advantage. It is important that making the inside outside encompasses strategies already taught as well as the strategy being taught in a lesson as this builds cognitive bridges across learning pathways in order to solidify knowledge into working and then long term memory. There are generally two models of thinking aloud: there is thinking aloud as an independent reader and there is invitational thinking aloud.

Independent thinking aloud is done without interruption solely by the teacher, from the questioning for clarification to the positive conclusion. It is commanded by the teacher's voice and acts as instruction for either new skills or to reinforce previous teaching in order to clarify misconceptions. In this model, the teacher wants all eyes on the process. It is no way intended to be a monologue – in fact it needs to be SMART in its use:

- Specific in terms of the skill deliberately being modelled
- Measurable in terms of text limitations, i.e. no more than one to a few sentences
- Achievable in that it is modelled in a way pupils can imitate
- Realistic in that it also demonstrates the challenges behind clarifying understanding and doesn't paint a simplistic picture of learning, bearing in mind the varied abilities of readers
- Time-specific in that the process is not grandiloquent or vague but concise and clear.

Invitational thinking aloud is done with the teacher's comprehension model as lead, with the child's thoughts solicited either to confirm or aid in clarification. By bringing the child reader into the modelled process, the teacher is moving beyond instruction to the metacognitive phase of gradual release. This process allows for the child to influence the outcome and therefore take accountability for their understanding while also developing the skill of reasoning. A main question is posed then several sub-questions ask for clarification at different levels, soliciting responses from individuals in the class therefore making *their* inside thoughts visible to the whole class. This model is a good formative assessment tool when deliberately demonstrating a misconception to see if pupils can regulate and correct themselves based on prior learning.

The following is an example of how independent and invitational thinking aloud can be done based on *The Raven* by Edgar Allan Poe (2016):

Independent reasoning and wondering aloud script

Text read aloud with a focus on language choice and effect on the reader	*Deep into that darkness peering, long I stood there wondering, fearing,* *Doubting, dreaming dreams no mortals ever dared to dream before;* *But the silence was unbroken, and the stillness gave no token,* *And the only word there spoken was the whispered word, "Lenore!"* *This I whispered, and an echo murmured back the word, "Lenore!"* *Merely this, and nothing more.* (Poe, 2016, page 4)
Re-read by section **Think aloud begins with a question focussed on skill**	*Deep into that darkness peering, long I stood there wondering, fearing…* Peering? I know that after hearing a knock he went to see who was at the door but what does the choice of the word 'peering' suggest?
Strategy recall	I wonder what peering means here? *'Deep into the darkness peering…'* (deliberate re-read to investigate the text). I could **read around the word** to see if the rest of the line can help me.
Strategy application	So… he's heard a knock and goes to the door to see who it is – I know this from the previous verse – and now he opens the door and it must be dark outside. I remember it was dark because it said it was midnight. So he is looking outside and it is dark. But the writer says 'deep into that darkness peering.' Looking deeply into the night? If you are looking deeply that means that you are really staring long and hard as if you are trying to find something and the line does carry on to say 'long I stood'. So 'peering' must mean he was staring into the darkness like he was searching for whoever may have knocked on his door, with his eyes most likely narrowed because he is trying to see into the dark.
Positive clarification	Peering gives me the impression that he was determined to find out who or what was at the door almost as if he really wanted to see the person he suspected it was. If the poet had said he was 'looking' it wouldn't be as intense as 'peering'!

Invitational reasoning and wondering aloud script

Continue to the next line of poetry **Question focussed on skill**	*Doubting, dreaming dreams no mortals ever dared to dream before;* (Poe, 2016, page 4) I wonder… What is the poet trying to tell us about the character's behaviour?
Strategy recall **Positive clarification** **Text investigation** **Additional questions posed to invite discussion focussed on clarifying** **Positive clarification** **Additional questions posed to invite discussion focussed on clarifying** **Positive clarification** **Strategy sorting**	Hmmm, first he was wondering – so he is thinking, I can imagine him saying 'what if it is…' and fearing – so he is afraid. Then he is doubting. If you are doubting something what does this mean? Like if I said I doubt what she told you happened in real life… [pause for pupils to pull from background knowledge] then it means that I don't… [deliberate pause and invitation to audience to **replace** with their own understanding]. [Interjection from a number of pupils aloud: Believe her!] Exactly! You knew what that meant so you could use your **replace** strategy right away. [Returns to think aloud process] So, he is intensely staring into the darkness, searching for maybe a particular person but at first he doesn't believe the person might be there. It then goes on to say *dreaming dreams no mortals ever dared to dream before* (text investigation). So first he's doubting, then he's dreaming. If you are dreaming about something, this can either mean that what is happening isn't real or what else could it mean if you are *dreaming dreams*? If I dream that one day I can become rich and famous then inside I am really not wanting it to be real? (deliberate use of misconception thrown into discussion for pupils to unpick using familiar context application) Do you agree with my understanding? Child A: No, it could mean that it is something you really wish for that may be hard to achieve… Or even impossible! Yes so he is *dreaming dreams* means he is hoping against possibilities or wishing for the impossible. It then says that *no mortals ever dared to dream before*. So based on what we already found out, he is saying that he is hoping for an impossibility. The word mortal – I have heard this word before! Have you heard this word before? [Child interjects: Yes. I have in Greek stories!] Can you remind me what it means? Child B: A mortal is someone who can die, a normal human being because an immortal is like a god who cannot die. Wow – that's right, well remembered. So he is saying nobody living has ever had this wish or desire for the impossible that he has at the moment. I wonder what this wish was. We will have to read on to find out. I think the writer is deliberately using different feelings in this one line. First it says he is *wondering* and *fearing* then *doubting*, and finally it says he is *dreaming*. If you are *doubting*, you said you don't believe in something but if you are *dreaming* then you need to be able to believe even if it isn't possible. Let us do some **positive-negative shade linking**. So if on one hand you are *doubting* and on the other you are *dreaming* then these are opposite feelings.

Strategy application	One is negative – which one?
	Child interjects: *Doubting* is negative.
	Yes. And dreaming is positive. I wonder if you can see any other positive-negative shades being used for his feelings from the line before. Let's look at the text. Oh – I see one more positive and one more negative – do you spot them?
	Child: Yes – *wondering* is positive and *fearing* is negative.
	So the writer is deliberately using opposite emotions. Why has he used opposites, I wonder? What does this suggest about the character's state of mind at the moment? (Teacher is now rounding up the think aloud to arrive at the fully clarified response linked to the original opening big question.)
	Child: If he is feeling two different emotions he must feel confused by his own thoughts.
	Hmmm – confused might be a bit vague but I see what you mean. I would say it is more like feeling conflicted.
Positive clarification linked to focus skill of original question posed	So the writer's choice of language – using negative and positive emotions – shows that he feels torn between his disbelief and his desire and is in a conflicted state of mind.

The invitational model is very much an interconnecting of what is already known and what is new and is a constant dialogue where the teacher still maintains the lead cognitive processes. There are elements of independent skill application, guided practice and rehearsal of strategies as well as modelling of how pre-taught strategies can be used to analyse text. Teachers can also assist with clarification to ensure pupils' understanding is fully developed. Essentially, the teacher always ends on the ideal response wanted from the pupils as a way of demonstrating how to tackle the skill being taught in the lesson. As you can see from the given script examples, there is no reason why both types of making the inside outside methods of questioning cannot be used one after the other in the same lesson as moving from independent to invitational reasoning is a way to transfer the skill to independent application.

6 Key strategies for building mastery in 2a, 2b, 2c and 2d domains

One thing I have observed with making pupils' comprehension visible for mastery is that their written responses often comes from a vulnerable place. Pupils are generally quite unsure about how to explain their understanding in writing due to a number of fears. These fears arise from a lack of confidence in understanding questions, understanding how to respond in written form and, of course, understanding vocabulary in the text itself. A key part of creating confident comprehenders is to empower them with strategies in order to simplify cognitive processes. This is about making apparent the smaller steps within each cognitive process and imparting this knowledge in child-friendly language that they will easily recall, understand and then apply. Becoming more aware of cognitive processes increases the probability that pupils will be able to more accurately create a written response. It is therefore essential that metacognition is the key focus of strategy teaching, the aim being to gradually release your need to scaffold and guide in order to enable independent 'visible comprehenders'. In the comprehension process, pupils need a sense of control in order to modulate both their thinking and their written responses. Therefore, it is essential to explicitly teach strategies in order for mastery to be achieved.

In teaching strategies, it is important to focus on the priority content domains, which make up the significant weighting for demonstrating mastery in comprehension, as well as those strategies that feed into these priority areas despite low test weighting. By focusing on these domains, the strategies will then become threaded throughout other areas of the reader's learning experience across subjects in the curriculum. Effective strategy teaching is about three things: explicitly teaching which strategies exist within a domain, when to use these strategies and how to use the strategies with efficacy. However, the essential thing here is timing. Strategy teaching must precede questioning around a text with the teacher first modelling the strategies before asking the pupils to put them in place. Although it is essential to teach strategies, with enough opportunity given to pupils to practice them, they will develop automaticity in application. At this stage, gradual release is necessary in line with the zone of proximal development. Strategy teaching is a lesson in itself which must be explicitly linked to a reading skill as a toolkit to tackle a particular domain focus. It must be embedded in context by working through text exemplars for it to be rendered necessary and it must be reasoned through aloud for its effectiveness to be demonstrated visibly to readers. The most important element of pre-teaching strategies is allowing pupils as much time as possible to practice the strategies being taught – by mirroring cognitive processes slowly at first and then at a faster pace when the opportunity arises in regular reading comprehension teaching.

Systematic approach to strategy teaching lessons

1 Make strategy to be learned explicit – skill introduction for particular domain

2 Make strategy purpose explicit

3 Provide context and read aloud

4 Make gaps in knowledge explicit

5 Demonstrate the strategy application with child-friendly terminology

6 Gap-fill knowledge using strategy reasoned through to accuracy

7 Vary context provided

8 Make gaps in knowledge explicit

9 Apply strategy – shared application

10 Gap-fill knowledge elicited from pupils

11 Present misconception explicitly

12 Check retention of strategy required

13 Investigate reasoning of how strategy is to be applied

14 Collaborate misconception correction

15 Elicit repaired response

16 Repeat the process until teacher input becomes unnecessary.

This process can all take place within a 30 minute session. Providing readers are exposed to various contexts within which to practice strategy application, the move towards automaticity will mean you are required to scaffold less, only needing to intervene where more challenging texts lead to errors. In that situation, you should use questioning in order to revisit the strategies learned.

Vocabulary and meaning strategies

For the purpose of teaching reading for mastery, it is important to provide pupils with opportunities to see the vocabulary strategies at play often. Getting them to work this cognitive muscle must be a daily occurrence with vocabulary always presented in context for them to clarify – be it as a warm up activity or throughout the lesson. As understanding vocabulary also relates to questions as well as text, bear in mind that the strategies will need to be demonstrated in both. There are three strategies that give pupils everything needed when it comes to clarifying meaning behind words; I refer to them as the 3Rs. The 3Rs are the **R**ead around the word strategy, the **R**oot word strategy and the **R**eplace the word strategy. These strategies are often taught in KS1 but somehow pupils coming up to KS2 struggle to know how and when to apply them.

Using relatable images for the 3Rs (see Figure 39) as a strategy prompt enhances recall and is something familiar to pupils who have been associating images with meaning since the early years. It also demonstrates to pupils how all of the three strategies work together in order to create a multi-layered methodology for tackling either new vocabulary or familiar vocabulary used in new ways. Often it is familiar vocabulary used differently which results in many misconceptions. For example – 'the boy ate a cheesy pie for dinner' as opposed to 'the boy found told a cheesy joke. 'Cheesy' is not a difficult word phonetically, nor would it be unfamiliar to a KS2 child. However, they would have to pay attention to the context in order to extract the correct understanding. Many times pupils will underestimate the

Figure 39: *The 3Rs strategy prompt chart*

need to apply a strategy in these instances but will readily note the need for them in order to understand vocabulary that is unfamiliar.

It is essential the strategies presented in the model (see Figure 39) are followed in order for the 3Rs to stick. The reason behind this is simply because the root word and read around the word strategy often complement each other and the replace strategy is ALWAYS used. By learning all strategies at first then seeing how each works independently and then how they work together, pupils are armed with the full toolkit to tackle most vocabulary they encounter. They can then play with the strategies at will until success is achieved. It is also imperative that pupils are shown where these strategies will not work – as in the case of technical words, archaic language and words in other languages where there is evidence of the meaning given within the text or not.

Read around the word strategy

When to use:

Use for a word that is strange or a known word used differently.

How to use:

1. Look for other known words in the sentence or close to the word we are trying to figure out. You can track backward by one sentence before the one which contains the word or read on one sentence after the word if more detail is needed to clarify. This is called the opened and closed sandwich approach.

<u>Open Sandwich (exploring intra-sentence meaning clues)</u>

From the beginning of the sentence   WORD   to the end of the owning sentence.

<u>Closed Sandwich (exploring inter-sentence meaning clues)</u>

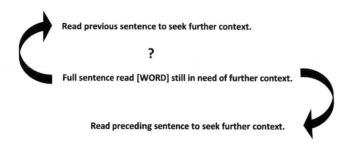

Read previous sentence to seek further context.

?

Full sentence read [WORD] still in need of further context.

Read preceding sentence to seek further context.

Figure 40: *Reading process for reading around words for meaning*

Both sub-strategies within the reading around the word strategy train pupils to re-read within parameters. Remind pupils that clues for vocabulary used in a specific context will usually be in close proximity to the sentence it is used in except where there is a clear indication in the text that the meaning can be found elsewhere, e.g. bold words found in a glossary at the end.

When not to use:

When the spelling conventions of the vocabulary to be clarified indicate that the root word strategy should be applied first.

Root word strategy

A root word is the smallest unit of vocabulary before a prefix or suffix is added.

When to use:

When a prefix or suffix is present that affects the meaning of the word, e.g. **mis**communica**tion**, or when a word is a compound word and a familiar word component can be identified as a root word within it. Compound words may be either hyphenated such as **cold-blooded** or closed such as **waistcoat**.

How to use:

Within the context of a sentence in order to check understanding.

Prefixed or suffixed words

1. Identify the root word where there is a prefix attached to determine familiar meaning in context.
    Context: There was *miscommunication* between the office and the staff that led to much confusion.
    Root word source: mis –(communica) tion = **communicate – to inform**
2. Link grammatical learning of the meanings of prefixes and how they change the meanings of the root word. Combine knowledge and interpret based on context.
    Prefix: mis- = wrong or bad – informing wrongly
3. Identify the root word where there is a suffix added which changes the word class to determine close synonyms for interpretation. Link grammatical learning of suffixes and linked word classes to determine what type of word it is. Combine knowledge and interpret.
    Suffix: -tion = noun – name = wrong information given

Compound words

1. Identify conventions of compound words. Split the familiar elements used on either side of a hyphen or within a closed compound.
    Context: The hunter looked **cold-blooded** as he approached the wolves with his sharpened axe dangling by his side. Although he wore only a **waistcoat** over his linen shirt, he didn't feel the cold from the bitter wintry breeze.
    Split elements: cold/blood   waist/coat
2. Determine familiar meanings of any or all of the smallest units of vocabulary, link meanings and combine knowledge to interpret.
    cold = no warmth + blood(ed) – not human, lifeless, no feelings
    waist = above hips on body + coat = worn outside of clothing – **short outerwear to the waistline**

When not to use:

If the root word is unfamiliar – regardless of whether or not a prefix or suffix is known – the root word strategy will not work. Use the context of the vocabulary and revert to the read around the word strategy.

The root word strategy is very much about lexico-grammatical awareness and teachers will need to build good knowledge of how morphology affects word meaning in order for pupils to apply this. It is pointless asking pupils to use the root word strategy if, for example, the spelling rules of '-tion' have not yet been taught for them to know the word is in fact a noun. Ensure there is a balance of this or model ahead to gap-fill where the text is operating beyond the grammatical teaching.

Note: Where the suffix of the word is '-es', 's' this does not affect meaning of the root word – it simply changes plurality. Where a suffix of the word is '-ed' or '-ing' this does not affect the meaning of the root word in most cases – it simply changes the tense and is a clue that it is an action (verb) unless acting as an adjective. The root word strategy does not need to be applied in these instances.

Replace the word strategy

When to use:

- Use the replace the word strategy to check if your understanding of a word makes sense. Replacing the word and re-reading the sentence to clarify meaning is the first step prior to writing or choosing answers. This strategy is a metacognitive regulator for increased accuracy.

- After applying other strategies and clarifying meaning, always use the replacing strategy to check understanding. Synonym words or phrases are necessary for any explanation of vocabulary to be in the pupils' own words or when they are selecting from options in a multiple-choice question. Essentially, replacing occurs when pupils give their interpretations of vocabulary meaning.

- When a synonym for vocabulary being clarified is already concrete from prior knowledge. Therefore, the replace strategy precedes all other strategies and pupils can clarify meaning immediately.

How to use:

1 When vocabulary is interpreted by the child, always revisit the text.

2 Remove the word or words being clarified and replace them with a word of their own understanding, i.e. re-read the text with their own word in its place.

3 Check if the sentence reads synonymously.

4 In the case of multiple-choice questions, take each option and apply the replace method until the closest in meaning is determined.

When not to use:

If own understanding has not yet been determined, replacing cannot take place. Pupils must already have determined a possible synonym word or phrase that might work within the context of the sentence.

Retrieval strategies

Retrieval is highly dependent on a child's ability to skim and scan as well as their ability to spot the key links between the question and the text in order to pull out the key details. The main misconception is over-retrieval (where too much information is recorded) or vague interpretations where text is paraphrased incorrectly.

The strike-off strategy

When to use:

To teach the difference between supporting and significant information during Phase 1 of skill lesson.

How to use:

The aim here is to visually strike off the supporting information, leaving key details untouched. Show the pupils what information you could remove as supporting details we do not need in order to know the who, the what, the when or the why. Reason aloud that simple conjunctions, verbs, adverbs and adverbial openers may not be needed and reinforce this with grammatical knowledge (i.e. adverbs tell us *how* something was done but we will still know *what* was done without this). Pull out and record the significant information read in the extract, making grammatical inflections (e.g. adding in transitory or modal verbs) or framing the key details into simple statements so the information flows and in order for recorded details to make sense to a reader.

Repeat the process with a further text example. This time, ask pupils which words need to be struck off. After each statement, have them verbalise the most significant details found. By saying it aloud, many pupils will automatically use grammatical frameworks for sense making.

Repeat the process with a final text example. Pupils independently strike off supporting information on their own copies of the extract. Pupils independently note the significant details found. Share responses as a whole class. Where misconceptions arise, the strategy fix question to ask is: 'Is there anything there you could remove?' Pupils will then re-read their responses and regulate their own errors by applying the strategy. This is the initial build-up strategy that feeds into summarising.

When not to use:

By Phase 2 children should not need to be using the strike off method. However it is still an excellent intervention strategy for children struggling to retrieve.

Skimming strategy

When to use:

To teach pupils how to skim read for key details during Phase 1 of teaching. The aim is to move pupils beyond the need to strike off supporting information but to use eye-tracking awareness to decipher the difference between key details and supporting information.

Figure 41: *Skimming tracking awareness*

How to use:

Provide pupils with a diagram of the left to right directional movement of the eye when skimming (see Figure 41). Emphasise that, when skimming, sight bounces quickly over supporting information (one or two words) between key vocabulary where it lands. Model the process with a paragraph by reading aloud key points while leaving out extra detail (a faster pace than normal reading as you are demonstrating the mental process of deciphering the most important information). Note the items the reader pick up by recording them separately for pupils to see. Revisit these notes and point out that you picked up on names in capitals, action words as well as common nouns. Draw attention to the fact that pronouns helped you to link key details to the aforementioned characters but don't need to be recorded. Only record significant adjectives from a noun phrase when there is no key action word present.

Verbally recount the key details in the form of a summary statement, modelling how key details lead to a big picture of the text.

When not to use:

This strategy is not suitable for close reading for specific information.

Scanning strategy

When to use:

To teach pupils to use scanning to deliberately seek information during Phase 2 of a lesson. The aim is for pupils develop an awareness of question-to-text vocabulary links.

How to use:

Introduce pupils to retrieval questions based on the previously explored texts. Ensure the questions move in chronological order to the text to first demonstrate the link in terms of sequencing of questions to order of text. Provide pupils with a diagram of the left to right directional movement of the eyes when scanning in a focused manner looking for specific information (see Figure 39). Emphasise that the eye darts across each line from left to right, often omitting several words or phrases until the linked text is found. Model the process of scanning for information from a retrieval question that has shared vocabulary with the example text. Annotate the word in the question which is the key subject to be scanned for. Ensure the question is adjacent to the text and model the parameters for the search for information which in this case would be first question, first few lines, the second question, then moves sequentially to the next few lines and so on. Model deliberately scanning for the key word from the question in the text, noting the spelling or grammatical convention, e.g. if the key word is a name, search for the capital letter that starts the name or if the key word is multisyllabic, look for long word shapes as opposed to short word shapes. Then model reading around key words to answer the question.

Repeat the process with more input from pupils. Finally, present a question where there is more than one area of the text to check to retrieve key details that are not necessarily close together in the text.

Add extra challenge by ensuring the key details are not necessarily in chronological order (i.e. pupils are required to track backwards). Keep the vocabulary in the question close to the wording of the text.

Vary the vocabulary of the question to progress to synonymous language contexts and overlap with vocabulary strategies in order to decipher similar language in the text. This time, apply the skimming and scanning strategies together, modelling how this is done. The key thing is to find something in the text which is similar in meaning to the key vocabulary in the question in order to determine where in the text the target information lies.

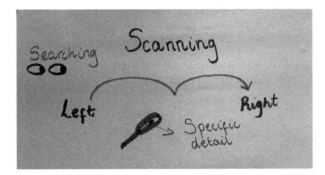

Figure 42: *Scanning tracking awareness diagram.*

When not to use:

This strategy is not to be used when developing summarising skills or where children are retelling text in sequence.

Find and copy strategy

When to use:

To sensitise pupils to recording specific detail only during Phase 2 of a lesson. The aim here is to gradually release pupils to independently apply retrieval and recording.

How to use:

Adapting 'find and copy' exercises is very useful for teaching pupils how to retrieve specific information. While find and copy questions often appear in the 2a (Vocabulary and meaning) domain, if used in the area of retrieval they emphasise the use of the exact wording of the text. Rather than asking pupils to 'find and copy words that show X', adapt these questions to 'find and copy specific numbers of words that give the key detail needed for the question'. By specifying what needs to be retrieved, you begin to train pupils to record within parameters. As pupils start to show more positive indications of the skill of exact retrieval, remove the find and copy instruction and ask more direct retrieval questions emphasising the 'find and copy' strategy. For example, find and copy the name of the country Tom travelled to after he left his home or find and copy two types of tools the Vikings used to repair the boat.

Vary the strategy to paraphrasing by noting when finding and copying does not make grammatical sense. The wording of the question needs to be as close to the text as possible. Model these examples, enabling pupils to move beyond basic word-for-word retrieval to close retrieval. The key phrase here is 'a strategy works until it doesn't' – but a strategy can be adapted so that it is still useful. Pupils can find the key details then reword for responses to make sense. This could mean moving information around, changing the tense or even using synonym words or phrases to match the key detail found in the text.

When not to use:

Avoid using this strategy where finding and copying exact wording does not work and readers will need to closely copy instead, changing some wording in the text for answers to make sense.

Retrieval strategy for group reading intervention

When to use:

For the purpose of intervention in a group setting, it is imperative that the cognitive steps are broken down in such a manner that teachers are guiding the thinking as well as the cognitive demand through questioning.

How to use:

Teach the steps with this child-friendly word play: UMCRAC – (U Must CRAC [said as *crack*]). Reinforce the meanings behind the memory prompt: U for Underline, M for Match, CRAC for Check Read Around and Copy (or closely copy). This gives pupils a clear scaffold to keep in mind when choosing which retrieval strategies they need to apply to any given question.

When practicing retrieval responses during Phase 1, teachers should make explicit reference to UMCRAC (see Figure 43) before simplifying the scaffold during Phase 2 (see Figure 44) until pupils become secure enough to have the scaffold completely removed.

SOS strategy

When to use:

The most common misconception pupils have when applying the skill of summarising is that most of their answer tends to be quotations from the text. Often pupils tend to retrieve and copy instead of finding the most concise manner in which to re-tell a text or an idea inferred from the text. To ensure pupils understand the importance of brief responses, the SOS strategy works very well. SOS can be taught as a child-friendly initialism, breaking down the cognitive processes like so: **significant** information; **own** words; and in the **shortest** way possible. The SOS strategy should be taught after pupils are secure using the strike off strategy in order for them to know what constitutes a significant or key detail. It should also be taught after the **3Rs** in order for pupils to be aware of using synonymous language after clarifying their own understanding. The sub-strategy of **shortest** way possible is the one in which pupils will need to be trained. Even when using their own language and just the significant details from the text, pupils will be guilty of adding unnecessary verbiage which can result in vague responses. Teaching pupils to edit and improve their own answers is key when learning to summarise as well as to use of parameters as a framework for structuring succinct responses. Start small – once pupils can securely summarise a sentence, you can move to larger chunks of texts and then on to whole texts.

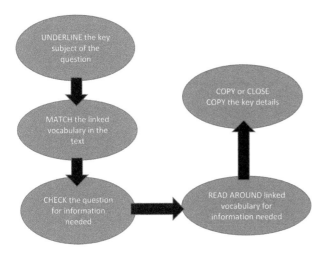

Figure 43: *Full scaffold for retrieval process*

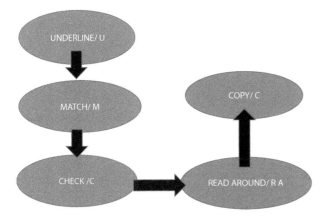

Figure 44: *Partial scaffold for retrieval process*

How to use:

Step 1

Provide pupils with one lengthy sentence from a text. Model annotating the significant details and rewriting in your own words but NOT in the shortest way possible. Revisit the sentence you've just created and think out loud about how it can be improved to be the most concise retelling. Strike off unnecessary vocabulary and improve your written response. Ask pupils to practise the strategy with a new sentence on whiteboards as a whole class. Assess for the best SOS response highlighting how you can see the pupils applying the strategy. Give others the chance to edit and improve their sentences. Where there are misconceptions, revisit the strategy using the cognitive processes as prompts and ask questions using the following script:

- Is that the most important detail that happens in the statement?

- Who or what is the statement about?

- What is the main action or event in the statement?

- Can you remove any information there and the important detail is still present?

Also challenge reasoning instructionally, e.g. *Show me where you used your own vocabulary. Identify where what you have written here relates to the text.* Repeat the process until pupils are actively using the self-check strategy (see Figure 42).

Step 2

Applying parameters to SOS responses is a challenging but often fun activity for pupils to practise their summarising. I always warn – if you ask the pupils to limit responses to a specific number of words and they struggle, ensure you have a best fit response ready to demonstrate that your request can be followed through. Provide pupils with a lengthy sentence from a text. Tell the pupils the parameters within which the significant details can be retold in the shortest way possible (e.g. eight words). Ask the pupils to write eight words on their whiteboards that capture the summary, ensuring it is structured with their own words where possible. Assess and challenge any misconceptions using the script from Step 1. Increase the challenge by sticking to the same text but redefining the parameters by asking pupils to rephrase the sentence into fewer words (e.g. five words). Pupils should challenge themselves to edit their original response to fit the new parameters. Tell them they are free to re-word with new vocabulary if the original statement cannot be edited to give grammatical sense.

Repeat the process for as much practice as is needed to build confidence. Pupils love this activity and see it as a kind of game of beat the teacher. I have cheekily dubbed it 'The Summarai Challenge' as they are 'chopping' out words they do not need.

Step 3

Provide pupils with a text broken into more than one paragraph and have them identify the key details in each through annotation. Adjacent to each paragraph, they should record the main ideas deduced from the significant information. Pupils need to use their own language to rewrite the paragraph but within

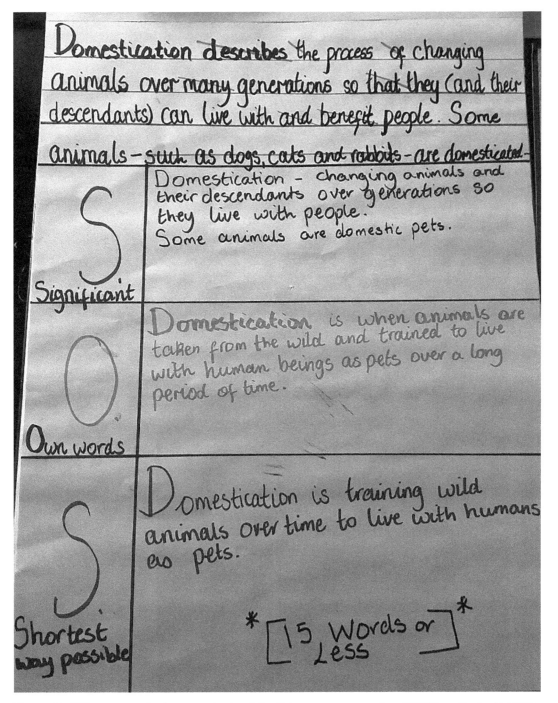

Domestication describes the process of changing animals over many generations so that they (and their descendants) can live with and benefit people. Some animals – such as dogs, cats and rabbits – are domesticated.

S. Significant

Domestication - changing animals and their descendants over generations so they live with people.
Some animals are domestic pets.

O. Own words

Domestication is when animals are taken from the wild and trained to live with human beings as pets over a long period of time.

S. Shortest way possible

Domestication is training wild animals over time to live with humans as pets.

[15 words or less]

Figure 45: *SOS strategy application example using Animal Management, extract from KS2 SATs reading booklet 2019*

a specified parameter, e.g. you should limit the number of words they are allowed to use. By positioning the original text and their annotations side-by-side, they can check to ensure the only things repeated are key nouns which cannot and should not be replaced and they can visually see the chronological order of their main ideas. At the end of the activity, pupils are to compile their summarised statements in a complete re-telling across the entire text. As a scaffold, main idea statements can be provided in the wrong order and pupils asked to correctly sequence them.

Inference and justification strategy

Many argue that inference cannot be taught as it relies wholly on the prior knowledge a child brings to a text which is often undetermined by the input of a teacher. To some extent this is a valid argument as background knowledge informs interpretations, but I believe that if pupils are taught how to visualise text, they will make more accurate inferences.

When to use:

Visualising text means that pupils need to see all the elements that appeal to their senses. How do writers create mental images that manifest in moving pictures of the imagination, filled with sound or silence, colour, action or stillness to name a few? All of which leads to the atmosphere of the text. The mood often changes according to events and character interactions. The work of Trevor Andrew Bryan, author of *The Art of Comprehension*, is truly inspirational when it comes to engaging pupils in deeper analysis of text through mood. He looks deeply at expanding visual literacy through the use of 'access lenses', mood structuring, and making connections through writing as a way of sensitising pupils to the similar things many writers deliberately do when it comes to creating atmosphere in a book. The strategy of the lenses is to present pupils with focal points in order to meaning make and put clues together to infer understanding. These 'access lenses' work wonderfully well as a strategy to build inference; the lenses are:

- facial expressions
- body language
- colours
- distance
- alone
- words or no words
- big things and little things
- zooming in or out
- symbols and metaphor. (Bryan, 2019)

As there are only nine lenses for pupils to be familiar with, they effectively remove cognitive overload by making all mood-enhancing elements of a text simple and accessible. In my own practice, I have found that they enable pupils to make structured inferences from any text type. It is highly recommended that teachers make use of these lenses as a key strategy for building strong inference.

How to use:

For example, where language in the text gives the reader information about a character's behaviour which acts as clues to their emotions, check to see if the clues are related to any of the lenses and use them alongside texts to prompt children to closely read for these clues. Likewise, when the mood of a text is affected by descriptions of setting, use lenses like the colour, big things little things or distance. It is important that teachers are aware of the mechanisms deliberately used by the writer to ensure they are able to guide children accordingly and select the appropriate lens. Where the writer uses figurative language in order to build comparisons to deepen the reader's understanding around a character or event, the 'symbols lens' is an excellent prompt.

Children should be encouraged to link any lens with the evidence in the text that creates an impression about the mood created. Ideally, the first use of the lenses should be in verbal discussion before moving on to documenting the exact evidence which leads them to infer their understanding.

Structuring written responses for justification strategy

When to use:

Once inferring is taking place verbally, the hurdle faced is teaching pupils how to justify their inferences. Justification sits right at the top of the Bloom's model within the cognitive process of evaluation. Teaching pupils to evaluate is very much about them firstly recognising a question to be evaluative through developing a sensitivity to the type of justification being required. Once this is soundly determined, the pupils have to know how to gather and classify information using the text as clues, decide on the best approach in order to respond and finally construct a written response. Therefore, it is imperative, for the following strategy to work, that pupils are taught the relationship between questions and answers. By using a processing chart, pupils become aware of what can be required of them in any comprehension question. The following processing chart is not to be confused with any other methodology of inference answers such as Point, Evidence, Explain, etc. or where all three are lumped together with different wording (though essentially the same meaning) for how to write a lengthy comprehension response. It is not intended to replace such preceding methods but to bring further clarity as to how a processing chart can be used with any comprehension answer zone. This chart is built for flexibility and, while useful for structuring written responses for inference, it can be used for all question types.

How to use

Introducing the processing chart (P-chart)

Purpose: To build a robust knowledge of question-answer relationships.

The aim here is to break down the cognitive processes that make up inference questions and responses. Pupils should develop automaticity in recognising the key elements evident from the processing chart. Hence increasing accuracy in structured written responses.

1. Explain to pupils there are three types of answers to questions which, when combined, can be used to make up a fully developed comprehension response. The three types of answers are **the reader's own opinion**; **evidence from the text**; and **an explanation of what evidence from the text means**.

2. Present pupils with the following processing chart (P-chart). Note that it looks like a maths number sentence for a reason – that is because the chart is meant to show how one or more elements are used to design questions and responses.

Figure 46: *P-chart formula*

3. Break apart the components of the answer chart to explain what each component means.

Figure 47: *First element of the P-chart.*

Your answer refers to the reader's opinion. It is a briefly summarised answer that shows what the reader understands from the events in a text. Explain to pupils that depending on how a question is formed, the reader does not always have to be them but can be presented as *a* reader's interpretation through a question.

because the text says"…"

Figure 48: *Second element of the P-chart*

This is a **retrieved quotation or close copying of a limited amount of text** which may link to a formed opinion as proof or may provide proof of specific factual information they need to make clear (e.g. when in the case of retrieving from non-fiction). Explain to pupils that evidence needs to be specific using the best evidence available. This is especially true when done to prove an opinion. Evidence also needs to be limited when providing factual information; there should be no unnecessary extra text before or after the evidence.

which means...

Figure 49: *Third element of the P-chart*

In this part of the P-chart, pupils should give their own understanding of the meaning of vocabulary used in the text or retrieved from the text. Teach the pupils that this type of answer can come in the form of explaining. To explain the meaning of text evidence (the arrow on the P-chart, which links the explanation to the evidence given) the pupils will rely on their **replace** strategy from the **3Rs**, ensuring they are using synonyms to the evidence given to show their full understanding. They should also be taught that when giving a fully developed response, the third element of the P-chart should not repeat any of the other information already given.

4. Provide a text extract with samples of related question types where each part of the processing chart is required. Ensure that the questions selected are focused on the domain area being taught – in this case, inference. Teach the pupils how to systematically recognise what is already present in each question. Here are examples of **P-chart** strategy lessons transcribed from sessions delivered to Year 6.

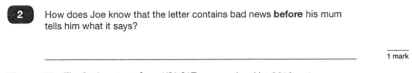

2   How does Joe know that the letter contains bad news **before** his mum tells him what it says?

_____   ‾‾‾‾
                                                           1 mark

Figure 50: *The Park, extract from KS2 SATs answer booklet 2019, p.4*

Teacher: Which part of the question tells you there is an opinion present? Look for vocabulary that has emotive words (words that describe feelings).

Child A: Where it says 'the letter contains bad news'.

Teacher: Is there text evidence present for us to explain in the question?

Child B: No evidence present.

Teacher: So is it necessary for us to give the meaning of any evidence?

Child B: No explanation necessary.

Teacher: Therefore we need to give evidence so we need the second part of the chart 'because the text says'. Notice that the question does not say to give specific evidence – this means we can use our close copying skills and are allowed to move words around to prove the opinion given in the question. (Teacher then refers to the text extract and reads the following aloud.)

brown envelope landed on the mat. 'Bit early for the post isn't it?' Mum said. 'Ooh, it says Special Delivery.' Mum opened it, and unfolded the letter.

Joe knew instantly that something was wrong. He could see it on Mum's face. 'What is it, Mum?' Joe asked.

Figure 51: *The Park, extract from KS2 SATs reading booklet 2019, p.4*

Teacher: So how does Joe know that the letter was bad news *before* she tells him? Remember we are focusing on the subject of the question which is Joe's mum.

Child C: He could see it on his mum's face.

Teacher: How else could we say this?

Child D: From his mum's facial expression.

Teacher: (Positive confirmation) Both are correct.

(Teacher then models for the pupils other ways this could be answered correctly using close copying.)

Refer to the P-chart explaining to the pupils that sometimes it can help them to realise which missing information they need to seek out in order to give an accurate response. Now discuss a different type of inference question for the text which gives the opportunity to apply this knowledge.

7 What is Joe's mother thinking after she reads the letter?

Tick **one** thought.

Figure 52: *The Park, extract from KS2 SATs answer booklet 2019, p.6*

Teacher: The question tells us that Joe's mother was thinking something after she read the letter. The answers are given for you to choose one thought. Look carefully at the language of the options. Are there any emotive thoughts? Let's read through each answer and annotate the emotive language where present.

The teacher then goes through the responses – circling accordingly (see Figure 53).

Figure 53: *The Park, extract from KS2 SATs mark scheme 2019, p.6, example of annotation*

Teacher: Even though three of these answers use emotive language, are they the reader's own opinion?

Child E: No, this is what the character might think, not the reader.

Teacher: Look carefully at this question which acts as a **locator** for us to find something out. A **locator** is not a type of answer but a direction for us to look in a particular place in the text. So what part of the P-chart do we already have in the question and the answer options?

Child A: We have a locator and what the mum might be thinking.

Teacher: So what do we need?

Child A: We need to find the evidence.

Teacher: Where should we look in the text for the evidence?

Child E: Where she is reading the letter.

Teacher: So there is no reader's opinion and the question isn't asking for one so we can ignore this part of the P-chart. (Teacher strikes it off visually.)

Teacher: The question gives us a locator to look for evidence so we complete the **because the text says...** Therefore, the answers must be the **which means...** part of the P-chart as the option we choose will explain our understanding of the vocabulary used in the text evidence. Now look at the answer we did not annotate. Would this be the correct thought based on the evidence in this text and can you give me a reason for your answer?

Child C: No it's not the correct thought because it was Joe who was thinking about the money his mum needed to cook the meal and that evidence is linked to Joe.

Teacher: Now that we know this answer is not correct, let us find the right evidence and review the other choices. We need to focus on the emotive vocabulary.

Teacher then refers to the extract and models scanning for the section after Mum has read the letter, then reads aloud.

'You leave that to me, I don't want you worrying.'
Mum tried to smile, but it didn't reach her eyes.
If she was trying to reassure Joe, it wasn't working.
He knew his mum needed that job – how else was
she supposed to put sweet-and-sour spaghetti
on the table?

Figure 54: *The Park, extract from KS2 SATs reading booklet 2019, p.4*

Teacher: Would Joe's mum be happy after reading the letter and how do you know?

Child F: No because in the previous section she had a worried look on her face.

Teacher: Ok, so this helps to eliminate another option. We now have two more and both are negative emotions. Which of these is closer to what Mum would be feeling? Let us **read around** the vocabulary in the extract to see if we can find a synonym match in the two answers left. (Teacher reads the extract with key details aloud.)

Teacher: (The text says …) 'You leave that to me, I don't want you worrying.' This could mean that Mum was worried – let us look at the option that says she was worried and read around that. (Teacher refers to response option.)

Figure 55: *Response option first explored*

Teacher: This thought says Mum is worried about the boys being late for school. According to the question, what has Mum just done?

Child B: She's just read a letter.

Teacher: So what will she be thinking about?

Child B: She's thinking about what was in the letter.

Teacher: So we can eliminate this option as there is no mention of being late for school straight after reading the letter.

(Teacher then refers to the text to check accuracy.)

Teacher: The next sentence in the text says *'You leave that to me, I don't want you worrying.'* Mum tried to smile, but it didn't reach her eyes.

If her smile didn't reach her eyes, what does this mean? Can someone show us how she might look while she smiled if it didn't reach her eyes? (Teacher makes use of collaborative learning through a knowledgeable peer who acts it out for others.)

Teacher: Explain what you just acted out.

Child A: I pretended to smile and just moved my lips so it wasn't a full smile just a little one so my eyes didn't move.

Teacher: So why did Mum pretend to smile to her sons?

Child B: She was trying to hide her feelings so she didn't upset them.

Teacher: So which of the four potential answers is correct?

Child E: The second option that says she didn't want the boys to realise she was upset. (Overall nodding from class in agreement.)

Teacher: Correct. Well done! (Ticks correct response.)

It is important that this process is repeated prior to tackling different styles of inference questions. By referring to the **P-chart** processes as a guide, pupils then develop automaticity in picking up both what is required of them to demonstrate their comprehension as well as what information the question already provides. It is a deliberately slow and methodological process which pays off. This is key when developing responses for inference, especially where pupils have to become familiar with the language of evaluation which is often quite emotive and packed with shades of meaning.

Systematic teaching guidance for inference

As inference can account for up to 50 per cent of the testable domains featured in SATs, it is little wonder that the teaching of inference often takes up the majority of lessons. We often use inference in our daily lives. However, many teachers find the teaching of inference quite overwhelming, especially as questions can be so varied and put a wide range of cognitive demand on pupils. Being aware of the different steps within the domain of inference can make a big difference to our understanding of it.

As inference responses are made of two general parts – opinions and evidence – it is important that pupils are familiar with the language of opinions and recognise that emotive vocabulary (the language of feelings) is the driver. Opinions are influenced by the information they read and can be justified as reasonable on the basis of closely linking their opinions with evidence. In other words, we can have differing opinions but the correctness of an opinion is based on how well it can be proven or which opinion is more likely based on the evidence present in the text. Evidence is purely what proof is present in the text that influences the reader's opinion. Evidence must be specific to avoid vague responses – and this is often the challenge as many pupils overwrite or give irrelevant evidence in the process of inferring. Summarising main ideas and retrieving key details are both skills that overlap with inference and justification.

For the purpose of whole-class teaching, we focus on the introductory (Phase 1) and then the core (Phase 2) skills of inference. The introductory skills always begins with looking at how well a child can gather evidence from a text. This leans heavily on their ability to retrieve key details.

Structuring written responses using the P-chart

For developing further structured responses, demonstrate questions where more than one of the elements of the P-chart becomes valid. For example:

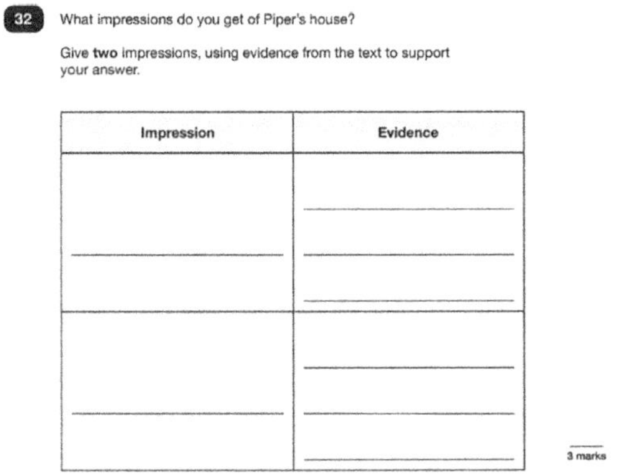
32 What impressions do you get of Piper's house?

Give **two** impressions, using evidence from the text to support your answer.

Impression	Evidence

3 marks

Figure 56: *Music Box, extract from KS2 SATs answer booklet 2019, p.16*

Ask pupils which elements of the P-chart are required and which are missing, as in the example from the script below.

Teacher: What is the subject or focus of this question?

Child A: Piper's house.

Teacher: What is an impression?

Child B: An impression is a thought in your head.

Teacher: So this is what the reader sees or feels? Which part of the P-chart deals with the reader's thoughts or feelings?

Child C: Your answer is about the reader's own opinion.

Teacher: The answer line is very short, so you need to summarise it in the shortest way possible. How many of the reader's own answers are needed?

Pupils: Two.

Teacher: (Clarifying) So they have to be two different opinions with two different pieces of evidence to support them. So which other part of the P-chart is needed?

Child D: Because the text says...

Teacher: Remember you do not need to write 'because the text says…' you can just **find and copy** the evidence to support your answer. Which part of the P-chart is not needed in this answer?

Child E: An explanation of the meaning of the text evidence. (Pupils then have a go at practising responses marked as a whole class.)

The clarifying of the elements aids pupils to think closely about how to structure their responses. However, in the Phase 2 period of teaching, the teacher deliberately does not model how to answer and moves pupils on to independently apply with partial scaffolding. The pupils are then provided with alternative styles of inference question which stretches the cognitive demand on them, as in Figure 57.

39 What impressions do you get of the relationship between Piper and Micah?

Give **two** impressions, supporting your answer with evidence from the text.

1. _____

_____

_____

2. _____

_____

_____   3 marks

Figure 57: *Music Box, extract from KS2 SATs answer booklet 2019, p.19, example of a developed response inference question*

Presenting this question to the pupils provides them with varied response zones (a list with longer multiple lines) to increase the familiarity of how more developed responses can be presented. Teachers will need to sensitise pupils to the layout of this question type, which implies a more developed statement is required for each answer. This particular style of inference question is closest to the old-fashioned 'big box' three-mark response but with some degree of structure provided to support the pupils as it is split across two points. Although the mark scheme for this question allows for pupils to support at least one answer with evidence, I always encourage teachers to teach pupils to do this twice, once for each point made.

Here are examples of what constitutes full-mark responses for this question type from the SATs 2019 mark scheme:

Award 3 marks for **two** acceptable points, at least **one** with evidence, e.g.

- *1. They were best buddies because it says she was pretending to be bothered by him though she was happy to see him.* [AP1 + evidence]

  2. They like to tease each other. [AP2]

- *1. They care about each other.* [AP1]

  2. They work together because he finds stuff and she fixes the stuff he finds. [AP3 + evidence]

- *1. They are good friends who like to banter with each other she says at the beginning she's 'stunned stiff.'* [AP2 + evidence]

  2. Piper seems to be the mature one. [AP5]

Figure 58: *Music Box, extract from KS2 SATs mark scheme 2019, p.28*

As you can see, as long as evidence exists in one statement, full marks are still awarded providing both statements also contain acceptable points. However, notice the format of what constitutes a well-structured response:

- *1. They were best buddies because it says she was pretending to be bothered by him though she was happy to see him.* [AP1 + evidence]

Figure 59: *Music Box, extract from KS2 SATs mark scheme 2019, p.28, demonstrating the P-chart structure*

Here you can clearly see the P-chart structure:

your answer – the child's opinion is 'they were best buddies'

because the text says… – the evidence is paraphrased as 'because it says she was pretending to be bothered by him'

which means… – the evidence is clarified as 'she was happy to see him'.

The second example demonstrates the same P-chart structure:

2. They work together because he finds stuff and she fixes the stuff he finds. [AP3 + evidence]

Figure 60: *Music Box, extract from KS2 SATs mark scheme 2019, p.28, demonstrating the P-chart structure*

Although this response is slightly less developed, the structure still remains balanced. The reader's own opinion, **your answer** from the P-chart, is present in the interpretation that the characters 'work together' and the element of **because the text says...** is present where the child uses close copying to say 'because he finds stuff and she fixes the stuff he finds'.

> • *1. They are good friends who like to banter with each other she says at the beginning she's 'stunned stiff.'* [AP2 + evidence]

Figure 61: *Music Box, extract from KS2 SATs mark scheme 2019, p.28, demonstrating the P-chart structure*

In the final example (Figure 61), the child has used a well-developed and well-structured response style. Here you can see the presence of the reader's own opinion where **your answer** says '[t]hey are good friends', there is exactly copied text for **because the text says...** *'stunned stiff'* and there is an explanation of the evidence **which means**, *'who like to banter with each other'.* Although not in the same order, the presence of all elements of the P-chart is apparent.

Essentially, when teaching well-structured comprehension responses for mastery, aiming for the well-developed response means that, should pupils come up a little short in the required detail, they will encapsulate most of the correct response. This is very much an 'aim for the stars, land on the clouds' approach. Essentially, for lengthier abstract answers that tend to carry three marks, the **P-chart** is to be encouraged to be used twice. **Your answer + because the text says... + which means... (evidence explained) x 2.**

The trickiest part of teaching pupils to fully develop their responses lies in the 'which means' element of the P-chart. The common misconception that pupils have is that they can simply repeat the opinion using a synonym. This is not the purpose of this element. The 'which means' part of the response is purely focused on the evidence and how this reinforces the reader's own opinion. Teaching pupils to copy text evidence using quotations means there is less likely to be errors introduced by paraphrasing – which is a new skill in itself. Reverting to **close copying** should also be taught and applied on those occasions where directly copying evidence does not make syntactic sense.

Repairing structure using the P-chart

Here are some examples of the process of teaching fully developed responses. The examples are taken from pupils who are developing their understanding of the P-chart for tackling inference as applied to the text *Letters from a Lighthouse* by Emma Carroll (2017). The responses are to the posed question 'What impression does Olive and Cliff give about the air raid shelter? Use evidence to support your answer'. Note the typical misconceptions that occur in the introduction phase and again in the development of gradual release phase.

> Cliff didn't like it because in the text it says "I don't like it Olive" Cliff muttered, which means he didn't like it. Olive didn't like it because in the text it says, "I don't like it either", which means Olive didn't like the air raid shelter.

Figure 62: *Misconception in well-developed response structure example Child A.*

These are common errors I have experienced over several years of practice. They are to be expected, as evaluative writing is a very difficult cognitive process which must be practised many times before mastery can be achieved.

In Figure 62, Child A is new to the use of the P-chart. The typical misconception is to constantly repeat evidence as their answer rather than giving a full response.

When this happens, the purpose of the **P-chart** elements must be revisited and particular attention should be paid to the **your answer** and the **which means…** elements of the **P-chart** response. By emphasising that there is no reader's voice if the quote is repeated (which means the skill demonstrated is simply retrieval and not inference), pupils will think harder about how they give their own opinion. By emphasising the replace strategy from the 3Rs for **which means…**, pupils will recognise the need for them to use synonymous language.

> They felt frightened and unsure because in the text it says "fought the urge to cover my head protecting with my arms" which means Olive is afraid of bombs. In the text it says, "I don't like it Olive" which means Cliff doesn't like the guns and aircrafts.

Figure 63: *Misconception in well-developed response structure example Child B.*

In Figure 63, Child B is starting to reflect on the **P-chart** processes carefully. They are now recalling and annotating the strategy to use from memory and are visibly applying it systematically. There is a clear opinion but this is not the opinion the child justifies. The mismatch renders the answer invalid. In addition, the evidence does not quite fit grammatically within the flow of the response. This child has over-retrieved, with two quotes not vastly different from each other, never mind the incorrect pronoun for Olive – a she. To correct this, the child will need to use the **close copy** strategy, i.e. remove the quote marks and re-word to make it syntactically fit. This was a clear case where it could be said that Olive and Cliff felt anxious as both said they didn't 'like' the air raid shelter. The child also needed to reflect on what not liking it meant in terms of the characters' implied preferences – they would prefer not to be there.

> They felt sad because "I don't like it, Olive" which means he didn't like going to an air raid shelter "I didn't like it either" which means she was feeling like Cliff.

Figure 64: *Misconception in well-developed response structure example Child C*

In Figure 64, Child C is showing more adherence to the P-chart structure, with only the second point showing repetition and lacking in-depth evidence from the text. A simple reminder to use the replace strategy to edit would improve this response. For example, 'Cliff doesn't like it' could have been replaced by 'Cliff was petrified of the guns and aircraft'. Likewise, the second quote could have been close copied for flow, e.g. 'Cliff was petrified of the guns and aircraft and told his sister he didn't like them.'

> He tried to be practical, a man instead of a boy tells us that Torak was trying to act like an adult. The text says, "he couldn't survive on his own" which means Torak thinks he still needs his father to help him.

Figure 65: *Well-developed response structure example by Child D, completed during the gradual release phase*

In Figure 65, Child D's example shows a well-developed structured response to a comprehension exercise done during the gradual release phase of teaching. The child is clearly manipulating the P-chart process which shows they have mastered its application. The **which means...** element presents first, followed by the **because the text says** and finally the reader's **own answer** appears last. This is perfectly fine as the response still flows and there is no repetition. There is now evident automaticity of the strategy which allows justification to be structured and sound.

The following offers a detailed systematic approach to breaking down inference into buildable blocks of evidence gathering and explanations. The guide is modelled on various extracts from rich KS2 texts but the principles could be applied to any text. Practice steps appear in the left column, with instructions and example transcripts from recordings of real life lessons on the right.

Mastery of justification

Context: *The Star Outside My Window* by Onjali Q. Raúf

   Learning Intention: To link given understanding to evidence from the text

   Aim: Begin by presenting pupils with an opinion based on a section of text that they have read. Ask them to prove whether what you have said is an accurate understanding by linking to the evidence which gave you the impression.

1. Teacher reads aloud then clarifies the response requirements 	***Text example: Mum would tell us to go to bed quickly because we could hear Dad's car [...] We had to race each other and pretend we had fallen asleep [...] so that Dad could see we hadn't broken any of his bedtime rules.*** (page 53) [Teacher: Hmmm…Pupils it is my impression that both Mum and the pupils were afraid of Dad and that he was extremely strict. Which pieces of evidence in this section of the text gave me this impression? Note I said *pieces* because I made two opinions. If I have two opinions, how many pieces of evidence do I need? That's right – two.]
2. Teacher looks for active engagement in extracting and classifying appropriate response	Pupils should look closely at the language and infer that the phrase 'bedtime rules' suggests there were other rules the character had not yet declared. A person with many rules about something as relaxed as bedtime ought to be would be inferred as being strict. Pupils would also look at the nuances of words like 'quickly' and 'race'. These words bring a sense of urgency and nervousness about being discovered which implies there would be consequences if the rules were broken.
3. Teacher enables pupils by ramping up or scaling back cognitive demand 	Depending on the ability of the class, this approach can either be scaled back so only one opinion is given at a time or ramped up in cognitive demand by asking pupils to prove multiple opinions. Teachers can also point out that the question is presented in such a way that the evidence can be found chronologically, i.e. the answer to the first question can be found in the first part of the text and so on.

4. Class practice of skill	Pupils should use note taking or informal writing opportunities to 'test out' their answers. The use of whiteboards here is encouraged as they give pupils the opportunity to restructure misconceptions, edit and improve responses after collaboration.
5. Collaboration and conferring	At this point, answers are shared. This could be teacher-led or child-led. Model answers can be used to help pupils see why these would be considered more accurate. Errors should be celebrated as an opportunity to learn how to edit and refine. This will be focused on ensuring evidence lifted from the text is specific and linked to the question. In a whole-class setting, make use of those pupils who are most confident in sharing their thoughts.
6. Teacher models how to answer	A key part of the process is to now model to the pupils how to correctly scribe responses. Use best examples or correct evidence to do this. This step can be skipped when pupils have shown their own ability to do this without assistance.
7. Mastery of justification demonstrated	When specific evidence is being recorded independently, pupils have mastered the ability to problem solve this particular question. **'Go to bed quickly** and **we had to race** shows us they were scared of Dad. **Bedtime rules** shows us that he was strict' is an acceptable answer when pupils are freely writing without a layout that has an answer zone line to match each question.

Mastery of demonstrating own understanding

Context: *The House with Chicken Legs* by Sophie Anderson

Learning Intention: To give own understanding based on evidence in the text

Aim: The next step is to flip the demand. This time, specific evidence is lifted from a text and pupils will have to give their opinions based on this. This is very much dependent on their ability to clarify the meaning of the vocabulary in the text and to associate context.

1. Teacher reads the question aloud. Teacher enables the pupils to answer by clarifying the response requirements and annotating the question 	***Text extract: Salma says '…maybe I'll get some more freedom …and to make friends with the living and maybe even shape a future of my own. My smile widens because for the first time …, I can picture a future in which I'd be happy.'*** ***Question: Give two impressions you get about Salma's life based on this text.*** (p.182) Teacher: Hmmm…the question asks for two impressions [underline in question] about whose life? Salma's. [Underline subject of response.] Looking at the evidence, can I identify two pieces of evidence that speaks about Salma's life? ***I'll get some more freedom*** [underline] this is one – can you spot another? [Gather ideas from the class] ***shape a future of my own*** [underline] is another. Anymore? ***a future in which I'd be happy.*** Oh yes! But that's three so we only need two of these to help us form opinions and they have to be two different and unique points. I think the first two quotes are related to one opinion I can form. What impressions do you get from these? [release the pupils for thought]
2. Teacher looks for active engagement in extracting and classifying appropriate responses 	Pupils should then look closely at the specified evidence and use this opportunity to think through what opinions they can form. Partner talk can be useful at this stage to help verbalise ideas. The teacher can then listen out for how answers are being extracted from the text and classified for appropriate responses.

3. Teacher enables pupils by mapping misconceptions and offering intervention prompts towards useful strategies 	Noting any misconceptions is key at this stage. How many pupils are repeating the text in their answer and not making use of Vocabulary and meaning skills (3Rs strategy) such as synonyms to demonstrate their understanding of the vocabulary? For example: Can you hear the evidence being repeated in your understanding? Do we need to repeat the evidence again or give our own opinion using our own words? Is it ok to simply say Salma doesn't feel free? Are free and freedom too similar? How else can we say exactly how she feels? So if she isn't free she is….? (Prompting for opposites)
4. Class practice of skill 	Focus on identifying good examples after pupils have had the chance to give it a go and bring these best examples to the fore and confer aloud. Ask the pupils what made them choose their answer . Verbal reasoning helps other pupils to pick up on ways to self-correct and refine their own answers while also developing their ability to justify their answers through speaking and listening.

5. Teacher models the responses required of different answer zones

	Present the pupils with different examples of questions where an opinion needs to be formed from evidence given but responses need to be laid out in different formats. Note that these are all asking for the same thing in different ways. Use standardised question formats, e.g. where the answer zone is presented as two long lines:
	Salma feels trapped and lonely. [2 marks]
	Explore the example responses in terms of how 'and' means you are adding a new main idea or linking two statements. Therefore 2 marks are easily earned.
	Also explore questions where the answer zone is presented as a list:
	    1. *She feels trapped.*
	    2. *She feels lonely.*
	Show the pupils how 'and' is not needed as answers are broken into two parts for two different points.

6. Mastery of own understanding demonstrated 	Give pupils two or three other examples of questions from a new chunk of text (no more than one paragraph) to demonstrate opinions with varied answer zones to show their mastery has been achieved.

This model should be repeated until reader confidence is sound, then you can simply remove the excess scaffolding in preparation for gradual release. Following this stage, it is time to move pupils on to the core learning of inference and justification. Asking pupils to prove or disprove opinions is a deeper level of analytical thinking – they will be doing several cognitive steps in this process:

1. They will listen to varying viewpoints.
2. They will refer to the text to form their own opinions.
3. They will compare their own ideas with the viewpoints received.
4. They will deduce whether or not they agree.
5. They will determine **why** they agree or not.
6. They will formulate their response mentally/verbally.
7. Finally they will write to master their argument.

Mastery of inferring using evidence

Learning intention: To justify an opinion with evidence from the text

Aim: This step is crucial in combining both opinion and evidence in preparation for written more structured inference responses. I often begin by doing this as a verbal debate which often whips them up into a frenzy, especially when I deliberately give them the most inaccurate opinion ever (we all know how pupils love to correct teacher errors).

1. Teacher reads the question aloud then engages in verbal reasoning 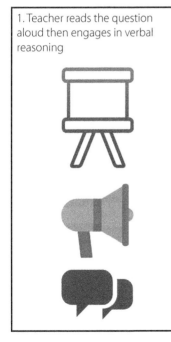	[Take a look at this quote from our book on the board from the chapter we read yesterday. I understand from this that ... (insert incorrect opinion). Am I correct in my understanding? Talk to your partner. I would love to hear your own opinions (give time for partner talk). OK – Ben I heard you say that Teacher is incorrect. What is your opinion? What evidence can you use to prove your response and prove me wrong? OK does anyone disagree? (question along same lines) Then round up by stating who was most convincing and gather the responses on the board while reflecting on accuracy. Yes I actually agree with Ben that I was incorrect. I think Ben's opinion that…. (write on the board) because the text says … Continue with another example – not necessarily incorrect and follow through in similar fashion.]

2. Teacher looks for active engagement in extracting and classifying appropriate responses	Pupils should actively engage in verbal reasoning or debate with partners or with the teacher. Look for pupils following through with evidence to back their opinions, noting who was more convincing based on evidence and how closely linked it was to their understanding. Question for 'going back to the drawing board' when pupils are short on reasoning ability, e.g. *Hmmm interesting, but I need a bit more to be convinced. I hear your thoughts but what proof do you have? Can you prove that? But that evidence you gave me tells me this instead, is there anything better to help prove what you say?*
3. Teacher enables pupils by ramping up or scaling back cognitive demand	Teachers can challenge and extend pupils by presenting more than one (but a maximum of three) opinions from which pupils can select the correct one and provide evidence for it, which increases demand. Another way is to vary the answer zone by asking them to simply tick the correct fully formed opinion as opposed to writing it out.
4. Class practice of skill	Pupils should use note taking or less formal writing opportunities to capture their reasoning. Use of whiteboards here is also encouraged.
5. Collaboration and conferring	At this point answers are shared and pupils take the lead. Pupils vote on which argument is the most convincing and also have the opportunity during this verbal share to edit, modify and refine responses. This is also a key opportunity for teacher assessment for learning.

6. Teacher models how to answer	Take an example of the most convincing opinion and evidence and place it on the board. Let pupils know the reasons it was successful. That you can see an answer 'No I don't agree', you can also see text evidence because the text says…' and you can also see that person's own opinion based on the evidence which means that …'. That these are the elements of a fully developed response for longer answers but will not always be needed depending on the question asked. At this stage you may vary the answer zone to demonstrate, e.g. showing SATs-style layouts such as two columns with impression versus evidence where an answer is not required, in preparation for the next lesson.
7. Mastery of inference using evidence from the text demonstrated	Move to mastery by providing pupils with a similar question in which they prove or disprove an opinion to complete independently.

7 Key strategies for building mastery in 2f and 2g domains

Seeing the patterns in text and effect

Teaching comprehension for mastery is about developing the deep analytical skills necessary for pupils to understand what they read. The aim of this section is to make the 2f and 2g reading content domains clear in terms of how to train pupils to be efficient meaning makers by looking at the tiny pieces of language and how they fit together to create the big picture. Language is like Lego® (see Figure 66); each component acts like a block that fits together to build a form of communication and whatever meaning the 'builder' or writer seeks to convey relies on all the components acting together in harmony. The teaching of content and meaning, as well as choice of language and effect, will enhance the reader's ability to infer from and analyse text. They act as catalysts to understanding and, by making the cognitive processes behind them apparent, reveal to the reader their purpose for meaning making.

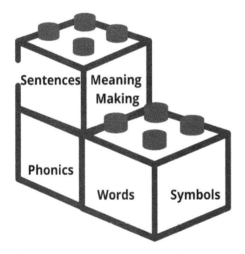

Figure 66: *Language components illustration*

Grammatical rules play a strong role in comprehension and automaticity by combining vocabulary and meaning as well as grammatical knowledge, providing the very foundation for reading comprehension mastery. Focusing on the smallest component of language gives an incomplete picture – which is why phonics alone doesn't work when it comes to comprehension and all pupils need to be in reading comprehension classes regardless of phonics ability. So what are the components of language and why do readers need to be aware of them?

The first block of language is the ability to decode. This phonetic awareness is essential in KS2 and, if not present, then it requires urgent add-on lessons and intervention. There is also the ability to put together graphemes then phonemes to read root words. As pupils acquire more root words and learn their meaning, they tend to categorise them in terms of word knowledge, e.g. are they synonyms for other words or opposites, are they verbs, adjectives, nouns, etc. There is also the ability to recognise how known words morph into 'new' words through the connection of root words and stems to prefixes and suffixes. Morphology implies meaning to readers in terms of word class, singularity or plurality and tense, e.g. -tion makes *celebration* a noun, telling us this is an event and not an action; -ed on the word *sprinted* tells us that this was done in the past moment; -s on *chocolates* tells us there were more than one; and 'will' added to a verb tells us this is the future likely possible action. Such are the foundation patterns of language which needs to be formed quickly and organically for a reader.

In the 2f domain (content and meaning), teachers need to focus less on the actual vocabulary used and more on the sophisticated patterns of word and text presentation. For example, do fonts vary in size or shape? Are they in italics, bold, underlined or in capitals? Do the fonts change shape with deliberation? What effect do these changes have on the reading experience? In terms of sentence structure, readers will need to be aware of the varying types, e.g. short, long, windy or broken, and why these are used. Then they should consider how those sentences appear on a page, e.g. are they read in a linear left-to-right fashion or are they written in a deliberate shape or alternate direction? Are they located in clusters across a page, under headings or beside symbols such as bullet points or numbers in lists?

Finally – what are the symbols between the words? How do these aid in the development of sentences and the meaning of those sentences? Punctuation recognition is a key part of comprehension which, when included as a critical part of reading teaching, empowers readers to grasp meaning making and fluency in a significant way. According to Trask (1997), 'if your reader has to wade through your strange punctuation, she will have trouble following your meaning; at worst, she may be genuinely unable to understand what you've written.' Trask said this as a warning to writers but raised equally solid points for reading comprehension. Punctuation shouldn't be taught only in the context of writing; it is a powerful part of analysing text and it deeply underpins the tone the writer chooses to set. The reading domain 2f (content and meaning) is a deeper one than simply being able to identify headings, subheadings, italics and bold writing. By KS2, pupils will be aware of some of the 'features' of a text type. They will know headings, subheadings, main titles, captions, bullet points and lists and it is quite easy to present them with a text where these are evident in order for them to annotate what they know. However, by KS2, pupils should be looking deeper at the purpose of further features with which they may not be as familiar, e.g. footnotes, call to actions, glossaries, charts, tables and graphs, labelled diagrams, references, etc. The role of the reading teacher is to present the pupils with varied genres and text types that allow for this exploration, so that the language patterns become familiar and pupils move through the different levels of awareness and understanding:

1. simply locating (Where is the main heading? This is the main heading.)

2. identifying (I know this is the main heading.)

3. recognising the purpose (The heading tells us what the entire text is about.)

4. looking deeply at the writer's techniques (the writer uses many short sentences) and the purpose of these (it creates a sense of urgency because the character is nervous.)

Use of lenses to analyse content

Presentation of language also includes the use of punctuation for meaning in writing. Symbolism through punctuation and presentation style is the hidden gem of good comprehension and yet it is often not taught.

Inspired by Trevor Andrew Bryan's access lenses, **content lenses** (see examples in Figure 67) have been developed as a key strategy to declutter the focus on content, making it easily accessible to pupils. Teachers can create their own lenses in order to enhance reader sensitivity to the things writers do deliberately, at word and sentence or whole-text level, to create meaning. The lenses in Figure 67 are main examples but certainly not exhaustive.

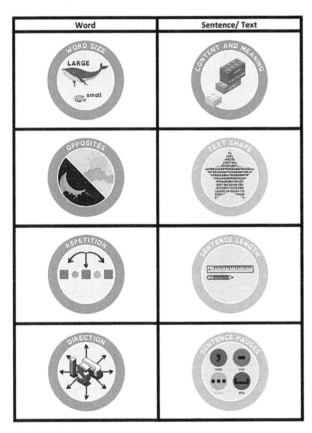

Figure 67: *Content lenses created for 2f lesson*

There are four word-level lenses to consider. The **size** lens looks at words deliberately made larger or smaller. The **patterns** lens looks at words deliberately being repeated. The **opposites lens** helps to identify words with opposite meanings deliberately juxtaposed in a sentence. The **direction** lens looks at words deliberately written at an angle, i.e. italics, or deliberately written to show movement across a page. There are also four sentence or whole-text-level lenses to consider. The **content and meaning lens** is used to introduce children to the idea of how the components of language work together to create meaning. The **shape** lens looks at how sentences may be written to form either an overall text type shape – such as a letter with address sections, a greeting line, etc. – or a shape poem. The **length** lens looks at the use of short or long sentences. The **pauses** lens looks at deliberate breaks in a sentence through the writer's use of punctuation. The lens includes prompts to address whether the pause is for an interruption of sound, a movement of time or when the writer is building up suspense.

Lenses act as a prompt for pupils to closely read while looking out for specific features without giving the answer away. They act as an enabling tool and are used primarily in Phase 1 of the teaching process. Once pupils start to notice details and independently refer to the lenses, they are no longer necessary and should then be removed as the pupils grow in confidence by Phase 2.

How to use content lenses

Below are several examples of teaching opportunities from various KS2 texts which demonstrate how to use the content lenses. The leading questioning scripts offer common patterns of language found in the classroom. You should feel free to adapt them to suit any other text chosen for teaching as the features discussed are used by other writers in many different genres, although for varying purposes.

Book: *Wonder* by R.J. Palacio	Extract: Part Five – Justin (Entire section)	Content lens prompt: Size Focus: • an absence of capital letters • an absence of speech marks except when quoting other characters
Leading questioning		• What do you notice is different about this section of the book? • What types of sentences are mostly used in this section? • When looking at the page, what does the absence of speech marks cause the text to appear like? • What do we know about this character? • Why has the writer deliberately done this for this character? • What does it tell us about his personality?
Pre-empted responses		Pupils with dyslexia will struggle to pick up on the missing capitals, etc. Clarify by saying that the feature we are looking for is something we always use to start a sentence or for the names of important places. You want pupils to notice that the sentences appear longer and in an almost run-on fashion as it is harder to distinguish beginnings of new ideas. As you read the text, you want them to notice the absence of speech marks when other characters communicate with the character and to also note that the character rarely responds verbally. They should notice that, apart from what we know are the character's own thoughts, he hardly has a voice heard by the wider world. You also want the pupils to note that Justin is quite an intelligent character – he uses a lot of technical words and retains much of what is said to him to be able to relay it to the reader. All of which leads up to what can be inferred about him: that he is very thoughtful, shy and quiet with a lot on his mind. His thoughts are so complex and there are so many that the style of writing suggests he simply has no time to punctuate properly or sees it as less important than what he wants to or chooses to remember and recount. (Many pupils will understand this from the times they forget to punctuate their own writing as they tried to get all their ideas out on paper.) After discussing the content and meaning, you may also link to useful background knowledge from the author himself to reinforce why he chose not to include speech marks and the impression he wished to create on the reader:

	'…when it came to writing from Justin's point of view, because he's a musician, someone who thinks in musical terms, it just seemed natural for me to use lowercase letters to represent his thoughts in a very visual way. He's the kind of person who doesn't talk a lot, because he's naturally shy, but has a lot going on inside.' (Palacio, 2012)
Misconception mapping	Pupils will need to be attuned to the artistic right of the writer to manipulate text and conventions in order to convey meaning. This means noticing that what is normally considered incorrect in grammatical presentation is done for a specific purpose in order to deepen characterisation or theme in a text.

Book: *Malamander* by Thomas Taylor	**Extract:** Pages 144–145 *Crack […] moving […] something Let go!*	**Content lens prompt: Direction** **Focus:** • italics for onomatopoeia • italics for thought • italics for emphasis of an emotion • italics for emphasis of a thought or repeated word
Leading questioning		• Can you identify where the writer has used italics on these two pages? Look closely at the first one, *crack*. • Why has the writer done this? • What feeling do you get when you read this word? • How did I read it? Why did I read it this way? • Now look at the next italic word *moving*. What did Vi do after she said this? • What did I do with my voice when I read it? • What do you think Vi is feeling at this point in the text? • What do these italics tell you as the reader about Vi? • Look at the next italic word *something*. Do we see his word anywhere else in this section? • Why is the other word not written in italics but this one is? • Listen to how I read it. What does this tell you about what the character is thinking or feeling? • Are these italics used in the same way as the other italic words we have read? • Now look at the final set of italics *Let's go!* How are these italics also different in purpose? • How is the character feeling now? • Where are these words taking place? So what do these italics show?
Pre-empted responses		For *crack*, look for responses that pick up on the sharpness of the sound and how the sound interrupted the quiet of the museum, i.e. the italics were used for onomatopoeia. For *moving*, look for responses that recognise there is an emphasis which suggests that in the closed museum it is out of the ordinary, in other words nothing should be moving. The italics here emphasise the emotion of surprise. For *something*, look for responses that note that it gives the impression they could not identify the object or that it was mysterious. Lead pupils to notice how many times the word *something* is repeated on the page before the italicised word is used and how this builds up the suspense because the writer wants you to notice the repetition. This suggests that the characters are growing increasingly curious to solve the mystery as to what it is. Italics is used for emphasis of the repeated word as well as the emotion of curiosity. For the final *Let go!* the italics are used for thought. The character is saying this in her mind but it also emphasises the emotion of desperation and great anxiety when her friend's life is at risk. Look for responses that suggest the impression is that she is screaming while noting she is unable to speak. The exclamatory sentence tells the reader the character is experiencing heightened emotions as she feels more and more nervous that her friend may become hurt or killed if she does not let go.

Misconception mapping	Pupils will need to go beyond thinking that italics are just for emphasis in order to explain what is being emphasised. They should also recognise that italics can be used not only to convey an emotion but also to separate different types of information in a text such as narrative voice and character thought.

Book: *Cogheart* by Peter Bunzl	Extract: Pages 124–25 *malheureusment [...] Désolée [...] ma chérie [...] C'est fini [...] C'est magnifique*	Content lens prompt: Size Focus: • Italics for separating types of information
Leading questioning		• We have seen italics before but look closely at these two pages. Which words are in italics? • What is the similarity between all of these words? • How do these italics differ from italics you have seen before? • Let us translate the words. Are any of them in italics also for another reason?
Pre-empted responses		Look for responses that note all the words in a different language are in italics or the words are all French. These italics separate them from the English words in the text. After translation, the only one with an added purpose is *c'est fini* as the character already said *there* as a one word sentence which means Madame is already convinced. So 'c'est fini', which means 'it is finished', is repeating or emphasising her mind is fully made up.
Misconception mapping		Pupils will become aware of the different types of information that may be put in italics. They will notice how italics can be used to help the reader to identify when information is repeated or built upon.

Book: *The Fox Girl and the White Gazelle* by Victoria Williamson	Extract: Pages 101–103 *...I swear I'll–* (page 101)... *I didn't...* (page 102) then *I'll... wait* (page 103).	Content lens prompt: Pause Focus: • Dashes for interruption • Ellipsis for omission of words • Ellipsis for interruption • Some reference to breaking lines for new speech and hyphens
Leading questioning		• Identify the dash on page 101. How does the dash look different from the hyphens used in the word *out-of-date* in the previous paragraph? • Who was speaking when the dash appears? • Who is speaking immediately after the dash in the text? Is it the same character? How do you know it isn't? • What do you think the writer is telling us by using a dash there? • Identify the ellipsis on page 102. What type of sentence is it a part of? • Who was speaking? • What happens immediately after the ellipsis? • What does the next phrase mean? • Is there anything else in this paragraph that tells us how our character is feeling at the moment? • Why didn't she finish her sentence? • What do the ellipsis suggest about how she feels? Why is it there? • On page 103, do you see any more ellipses? • Is this ellipsis used in the same way? Did anyone else speak? How is it different? • Is there another dash on this page? Is it used in the same way as the dash we saw before? How do you know?

Pre-empted responses	You are wanting pupils to pick up on the stylistic convention that a dash is longer and usually appears in the middle of or at the end of a sentence, while a hyphen is shorter and joins words together. They should also notice that it occurs in a speech sentence before Caylin finishes speaking and we know she has not finished because it is not an 'end' punctuation like a full stop, question mark or an exclamation point. It suggests more was there to be said. The new character, Reema, begins speaking immediately after the dash. It is a new character because the speech sentence appears on a new line. This implies that Reema stopped Caylin from finishing her sentence. The dash tells the reader Caylin was interrupted and it also suggests that Reema is annoyed or angry as she did not wait to hear what Caylin had to say.
	The ellipsis is also a part of a speech sentence and is used when Caylin was trying to explain. The text tells us after that she trailed off. This means that she stopped speaking mid-sentence. The text also says that *the fight was knocked out of her*. This means she had given up. The ellipsis tells us she didn't finish speaking because she couldn't be bothered or was tired of arguing to defend herself, which implies she didn't think it would make much difference. The ellipsis means words are missing because she chose not to speak anymore. The next ellipsis is not used in the same way. Although words are missing and Caylin chose not to finish her sentence, she is still speaking. She changed her mind about what she wanted to say. This one shows that her original thoughts were interrupted by what Reema told her. The dying and sick cub became more important for Caylin to focus on. The ellipsis shows an interruption of thought and introduces a new thought. This suggests that Caylin was worrying about her decision and whether or not Reema was correct.
	The dash is used in the same way as before but this time the interruption is not someone else speaking but a familiar sound. This interruption to listen suggests it was more important to identify who was coming and that Caylin was now nervous.
Misconception mapping	Pupils will see that more than one punctuation mark can be used for similar effect while exploring what they can infer from the symbols. They will go beyond the concept of a dash being used for parenthesis instead of brackets or commas and ellipsis being used as a cliff-hanger.

Book:	Extract:	Content lens prompt: Size
The Many Worlds of Albie Bright by Christopher Edge	Page 49 *CERN… USB… DECAYED ACTIVATION AT BEAMPIPE ETC…*	**Focus:** • Use of capitals for acronyms • Use of capitals for style
Leading questioning	• Where can you see capitals used differently on this page? • What do these capitals mean? • Is this how we have always seen words in all capitals used in other texts? • Are all the capitals on this page used in the same way? • Where are they used differently? • How have they been used differently? • What impression does the use of capitals give you about this part of the story?	

Pre-empted responses	You are looking for answers where pupils pick up on the use of acronyms. Where prior knowledge of the technical acronyms is absent you should present this through images, e.g. picture of a USB stick, and the words for the acronym to enhance their understanding, with simple explanations of the use of a USB as opposed to encouraging knowledge of the vocabulary itself. The idea here is to inform the reader that often technical words are written this way. You are looking for pupils to reflect on previous learning where capitals are used for shouting or loud noises, which is not the case in this section of text. They should also be able to categorise acronyms separately from the technical vocabulary in capitals which is being read from the *computer printouts*. That the final set of capitals are different because the writer is showing the reader how the letters appeared on the printout that the character read. You are looking for the pupils to recognise that the text is focused on quantum physics which the character struggles to understand so it makes sense that the reader may be confused too.
Misconception mapping	Pupils move beyond understanding all capitals as shouting or used for onomatopoeia to learning that capitals can be used to abbreviate longer words or to mimic things the character sees.

Book: *A Monster Calls* by Patrick Ness	**Extract:** Pages 26–27	**Content lens prompt: Pauses** **Focus:** • Use of spacing and symbols between paragraphs or sections of text
Leading questioning		• How can we tell where the chapter begins? • How can we tell when a new paragraph begins on the page? • Have we seen this done differently in other books? • On page 26 there are some symbols before the first paragraph. What happened before these symbols? • What happened after the symbols appeared? • Why are they there? • Is there any paragraph on page 27 that seems further away from the previous paragraphs? • What was happening in the paragraph before this space? • What was happening in the paragraph after this space? • How was Conor feeling in the paragraph before the space happened? • Why has the writer made the space larger than just a regular line skipped for a new paragraph?
Pre-empted responses		Look for responses that note that in this text each new paragraph is indented and on a new line whereas in other books there may not be an indentation. Look for pupils re-telling that the character was dreaming before the three dots and woke up to reality after these symbols on the page. Note that the symbols therefore meant this was really where the true events begin and mark a new type of beginning for the boy's morning but not the beginning of the chapter. Look for responses where the pupils note that Conor was alone in the previous paragraphs preparing to go to school and doing his chores and that, after the longer space, his mother appeared. Pupils should also note that while alone he seemed uneasy or was anxiously watching the time and worrying about his mother not being there. The longer space suggests her being there was a big deal, or maybe unexpected as he had so many responsibilities it seems he was used to being on his own. It suggests that Conor may have been surprised or that this was a new event for him as even in his dream he was eating breakfast alone and he expected her to not be in the kitchen but in bed.
Misconception mapping		You are deliberately looking for pupils picking up on the different but deliberate way new events can appear on the page by drawing their attention from the things they already know (a chapter title and what was read) to things they may take for granted – how paragraphs are marked, the use of a dinkus, i.e. three dots or spaces.

Book: *Saffy's Angel* by Hilary McKay	Extract: Pages 76 – 78	Content lens prompt: Sentence Length **Focus:** • Use of short sentences
Leading questioning	\multicolumn{2}{l|}{• Look at page 76. Do any sentences appear differently than the rest on this page? Which stand out? • Who is speaking on each line? • How do you know without any description that there are two speakers? • Why do you think the two characters spoke this way to each other? • Is there any suspense here? • Look at pages 77 to 78. Are there any other short sentences? • What types of short sentences are they? • What impression is created by having so many short sentences on the same page? • How does Saffron feel during this conversation? • How does Sarah feel during this conversation? • How has the writer's use of several short sentences helped the reader to understand how the girls feel at this point in the text?}	
Pre-empted responses	\multicolumn{2}{l|}{Look for pupils spotting the series of short sentences and identifying that it is a conversation between Saffron and Sarah, because the previous paragraph shows Sarah asking a question which Saffron answers on the next line. Sarah is questioning Saffron repeatedly because she is trying to find out if Saffron is of any use to her and so might be feeling slightly frustrated with Saffron's responses. Saffron's short answers implies she may be embarrassed about not knowing how to help Sarah with her homework subjects. There is no suspense present. The several short sentences are a mix between exclamation sentences and questions. You can tell from the several exclamation marks that both characters are getting worked up. It gives the impression that the conversation is intense and there is a build-up of Saffron's curiosity and Sarah's annoyance. It also gives the impression that Saffron is talking rapidly and hardly giving Sarah any time to communicate. This is reinforced when her several questions are met with no answer by the end of the conversation.}	
Misconception mapping	\multicolumn{2}{l|}{Pupils will go beyond seeing short sentences as just a build-up of suspense to see that writers can use them to create a sense of urgency, curiosity or tension. In this case, the short sentences create tension based on Sarah's agitation.}	

Choice of language lenses

Lenses can also be created to enable pupils to focus on clarifying their emotive responses to positive, negative or neutral moods derived from shades of meaning (see Figure 63). Plotting words on a graph which measures intensity of meaning is a common strategy, but the difficulty in interpreting the author's intent by language choice often comes from defining the emotion felt. Vocabulary that clearly defines the different emotions should be built up during comprehension sessions as the mood presents or changes. The **mood lenses** can be used to prompt pupils to identify the type of language in a text which will impact on their reader reactions. Pupils should be asked what language is used to describe what they hear, see, smell, or what something feels like as the opportunity arises in order to refine emotive connections to the reader from the text.

The **emotive lenses** are a prompt for inward reflection. This should always be linked to text evidence and specific words that create a given effect on the reader should be highlighted and described. When pupils begin to define their emotions with greater accuracy, the vague response describing choice of language as 'for effect' diminishes. Always emphasise *what* the effect is as well as *how* the effect is achieved simultaneously. This gives purpose to language choice and also aids pupils' developing ability to infer.

Figure 68: *Emotive and mood lenses created for 2g*

8 Book talk-ability sample lessons for 30-minute group reading interventions

The concept of book talk-ability in group reading is based on a fusion of informal book talk; skill building through developing question-answer relationships using standardised language as well as domain content focus; and collaborative learning. The sole purpose of group reading is teach strategies around domain content learning and application. Figure 69 demonstrates how the intervention model of group reading should look in practice. It is essential that all grouped pupils be reintegrated into whole-class reading comprehension lessons once gaps are duly plugged.

Figure 69: *Group-reading intervention model*

In this chapter, you will find sample lessons based on work with over 100 Year 5 and Year 6 pupils over three years of delivery. All of these pupils achieved expected standards in their tests, with a significant percentage achieving greater depth as a result of the intervention. Each group contained a maximum of 10 pupils who were worked with on average twice a week from September to May in the case of

Year 6 and from September to June for Year 5. These models have also proven to work in as short a time as December to May leading up to the SATs test for Year 6.

For the purpose of clarity, the lessons are split into full block units of six weeks per text. The flow is systematic and covers the full range of testable domains for the SATs reading test. Note that these lesson plans can be used with a variety of text types. The aim of this section is to show how organically the strategies outlined in this book work within a group setting purely designed for intervention or boosting comprehension skills. The lesson plans do not replace whole-class teaching where the strategies are also reinforced. Strategies taught in group reading must link to those used in whole-class teaching; if they are used in isolation, their impact will be reduced. All pupils of all abilities must be taught the strategies to tackle text analysis.

In addition to the lesson content, each sample lesson provides a list of the main misconceptions that I have encountered when delivering these sessions. Misconception mapping is a key element of preparation when teaching group reading as it ensures the teacher is as prepared as possible to successfully unravel any misconceptions the pupils may have.

Generally, these sessions use the same resources. Provide each child with a whiteboard and whiteboard pen; the teacher should use either a classroom whiteboard or flipchart for demonstrating strategies or recording responses. Where additional resources are required, they are also outlined below. Each 30-minute session is part of a block of six lessons based on the texts used. Included is an outline of the session focus, question stems and examples linked to the learning focus. Most sessions include a round up which either reinforces the learning from the session or acts as formative assessment for the session to come. It is important to note that although not stated, there must be time dedicated to the teacher reading aloud at the start of each session. The teacher should read aloud on average the first two pages of longer chapters or at least one page before going into the teaching. You can also use this opportunity to listen to at least two children read to check for fluency within the first ten minutes of sessions that are less cognitively demanding. Where this is possible, a read aloud icon is indicated below.

Year 5

Book used for sessions: *The Unluckiest Boy in the World* by Andrew Norriss

Session 1: Making predictions and applying inference

Aim: To activate prior knowledge, make links to own experience, make links to texts and make links between pictures/objects

Resources: Mystery box containing pictures/objects

Lesson content: Identify each picture/object in the mystery box and discuss what the pupils know about each item. Explore how each item could it be connected to the text you are about to read. Compare items for links and pull on any previous experience of them that may exist in the class. Predict what type of text the class is about to read.

Key questions:

Why do you think the illustrator chose this picture/text/font/colour?

What do you know about…?

How do these link together?

What could the book be about?

What does ……. mean?

What type/genre of story is it?

Read blurb/find the author. Have you read any other books by this author?

Have you read any other adventure stories?

If pupils do not have the necessary background knowledge, provide them with pictures of the vocabulary or bring objects to help explain.

Round up: Why was Nicholas worried about his mother?

Session 2: Applying vocabulary strategies

Aim: To introduce the 3Rs

Extract: Pages 1 - 23

Resources: 3Rs chart (see p.81)

Lesson content: Introduce the 3Rs as strategies to help us figure out the meaning of unfamiliar words or words we know that are used in unfamiliar ways. Place vocabulary from the text on display, e.g. *misfortune, dog your path, enmity, dramatic, delayed, filtering equipment, mechanical failures*. Read the focus vocabulary aloud to the pupils and explain we will come across these words in the extract used in the lesson (it isn't important if you do not complete the extract as long as you get to the vocabulary chosen). Check if they know the meaning of the vocabulary you are targeting by presenting it in an accessible sentence for context. Explain that you will be showing them how to use the 3Rs to figure out new words in the context of the text. Demonstrate applying the strategy to two of the sentences in the extract. Pupils should do 'thumbs up' when they spot the noted vocabulary in the text as you read the chapters aloud (this tracks fluency and listening skills).

Demonstrate how to choose between the 3Rs strategies when encountering key vocabulary in the text. For example, 'misfortune': the root word is the priority strategy because you can see a prefix and a root word. Fortune means 'luck' in this case. The prefix mis- means 'bad'. Putting both my meanings together, I can explain that 'misfortune' means 'bad luck'.

After the root word strategy has been applied, move on to the phrase 'misfortune dog your path'. Demonstrate the read around strategy, noting that reading around is not only about the sentence the word appears in but also about reading around knowledge, e.g. What else do we know about dogs? Have you ever walked along a path and a dog comes to meet you? How does the dog behave? It is important that scenario you use enables pupils to decipher the meaning of the word or phrase you are targeting and is not just general knowledge. This is about modelling appropriate context. Get the pupils to see what you want them to see – a dog wrapping itself around someone's legs in desperation for attention and the person almost tripping over the dog. Then lead the pupils back to the text to link what they have just learned about the phrase; if misfortune is dogging the path of the character, then bad luck is constantly in the way or constantly stopping their progress.

Model how to replace the target word or phrase synonyms and explain that this is the replace strategy: in order for meaning to be clarified, you have to use your own words to show your understanding. Also demonstrate placing the interpreted meaning back into the text to replace the original words, therefore also showing that the replace strategy is also about sense making, e.g. bad luck was constantly following Nicholas Frith wherever he went. Does our understanding make sense in the context of the rest of the text?

Make it clear to the pupils that the 3Rs can be used interchangeably but they should choose a priority strategy based on the presence of clues, e.g. the presence of prefixes, suffixes or compound words implies that the root word strategy is the best fit and other strategies can follow after if needed.

Key questions:

Take a look at this word or phrase in the sentence I have just read. Which strategy do you think I should use to figure it out? (You can encourage pupils to write the 3Rs on their boards in a list format to remind them of the strategies they have available to them.)
Can you explain why you chose that strategy and how it would work? (Target specific pupils.)
What meaning did you get by applying that strategy?

Misconception mapping:

Look out for pupils randomly choosing strategies without a reason. Encourage them to refine their thinking and make sure they are critical of their choice. Make it clear you intend to ask them to prove how their strategy works – this will minimise guessing. Use questioning to help to remove misconceptions and redirect thought in order for pupils to arrive at the correct choice.

Round up: What are the 3Rs again? When do we use them? When don't we use them?

<u>Session 3</u>: Retrieving and recording key information

Aim: To recognise the difference between supporting information and significant detail

Extract: Pages 24–38

Resources: Photocopied extracts (pages 32–35) for pupils to annotate

Lesson content: Explain to pupils that in order to retrieve, they need to know the difference between supporting information, key details and main ideas. They need to see the supporting information as descriptive language and extra detail; key details are the significant persons, things, places and actions;

and the main idea is the summary of the most important information taken away from a section of or from the whole text.

Place a paragraph from the extract from the book you are reading on the board, e.g. *The boy was extremely unlucky from the moment he was born*. Systematically strike off the supporting information. ~~The~~ boy ~~was extremely~~ unlucky from ~~the moment he was~~ born. Explain to the pupils that the details you have removed add structure and description to the key details and the key details are likely to be the parts they will receive retrieval questions about. A question like 'How did the boy feel?' could be answered simply with one word – 'unlucky'. Acceptable retrieval responses for 'When did he feel his bad luck began?' would be 'from birth' or 'from when he was born'. Explain that it would be unnecessary, although not incorrect, to repeat the full phrase 'from the moment he was born'. This modelling makes pupils faster at retrieval, more specific and therefore able to move on to more challenging responses. Repeat this modelling with up to three other statements in the same paragraph. Get pupils to note down on their whiteboards the key details of each sentence in the text until the paragraph is complete. At the end of this activity, ask pupils to summarise the main idea of the paragraph in preparation for the next session.

Key questions:

What information can we remove?

Do we need that pronoun or is there a name there that tells us who it is about?

Can we take out the adverbs and still know what action took place? Do we need that adverb to know that he ran, for example?

Can you make a note of the most important thing that happened in this sentence and to whom?

Misconception mapping: Look for pupils adding supporting detail and prepare to refine their responses with questioning. Look for pupils giving the main ideas instead of key detail; explain that this stage is about using the exact language taken from the text (or as close as possible).

Round up: What was this section of text about? Can you give the main idea in your own words? (The second question will act as a formative assessment for the next session.)

Session 4: Summarising and sequencing events

Aim: To show pupils the link between the main idea and the ability to recount a text using summarised statements. To develop their ability to sequence a text using summarised statements.

Extract: Pages 39 - 49

Resources: Photocopied extracts for pupils to annotate

Lesson content: Take a section of the text and extract four key sentences. Jumble up the order of the sentences. Write these on the board and place letters A to D beside each statement.

Revisit the previous lesson and check the skill retention: make sure pupils know the difference between key details and the main idea. Reflect on the use of the Replace strategy where we use our own words to retell the main idea.

Explain to the pupils that the sentences on the board are the main ideas for the text they are about to hear but there is a problem with them as they are not in the right order. Their task is to re-order the statements correctly. Read aloud no more than five paragraphs of the text. Model annotating the first paragraph on a photocopy to find the main idea, checking against the statements on the board then noting the number 1 beside it as first in the sequence. Underline the key details in each statement as you progress through the sentence. Thinking aloud is key for this process. Also model pulling out the main idea using synonym phrases but not replacing the main nouns, noting that these are significant.

Key questions:

Now that we have read another paragraph, read the rest of the summary statements on the board. Which one is next? Write each of the summary statements beside the matching paragraph on your handout.
Can you now label the statements from 1 to 4 to show the order they appear in the text?

Misconception mapping: Pupils may struggle with synonyms the teacher uses in the summarised statements. When this happens, go back to annotating key details in sentences and ensuring pupils remember the difference between supporting information and key detail. Revisit the replace strategy by looking closely at a statement the pupils are struggling with and seeing how the ideas in that summary statement connects in meaning to key details in a paragraph.

Round up: Can we give one statement giving the main idea of the entire section of the text we read today? Have a go at quickly writing one on your whiteboards.

Session 5: Demonstrating inference through forming opinions

Aims: To sensitise pupils to the language of evaluation through expressing feelings or emotions deduced from the actions and descriptions of characters in a text

To identify when an opinion is required from inference question types that do not require justification with evidence

Extract: Pages 39–49

Resources: A mood lens poster or slide for the board

Lesson content: Read aloud to the group the next section of your text (up to two pages). Revisit each paragraph and question around vocabulary and meaning for preselected words and phrases. Ensure pupils are remembering to apply the 3Rs. Discuss any meanings that the pupils find difficult. As a rule, cover no more than three words and two phrases in a session. If there is any other tricky vocabulary, explicitly teach the meaning of the vocabulary to enable pupils to add it to their repertoire; use images where possible to make the learning concrete, e.g. provide an image of the *recovery position* so they can visualise what a *casualty* is from the text. Move on to exploring the descriptions and behaviours around a character using positive and negative language. Explain that the words chosen by the writer can give a positive or negative mood (refer to the lenses, p.92, but remove the neutral option) and that many times the language shows us these impressions without being explicit and it is our role as skilled readers to pick up on the negative and positive moods in the text. For example, in *The Unluckiest Boy in the World*, when the main character sees strange symbols on the large rock; the reaction of the driver and the mother when Nicholas has his accident; and the hidden nature of the body in the tomb – all of these descriptions and actions tell us that the event was a negative one. For every section where a negative or positive opinion can be formed, question it systematically and categorise it using mood lenses. The aim is to squeeze all the emotions out of the text. Revisit each statement where this is a possibility, ensuring all pupils have the chance to share an opinion about Nicholas or the other characters and tell you themselves if it is a negative or positive opinion. Start questioning by offering your own understanding then move pupils quickly on to giving their own opinions.

Key questions:

How does this text (read quote) suggest that the character felt (insert emotive language)? Avoid simplistic language like 'sad, happy, upset'; model descriptive of higher level emotions, e.g. devastated, joyous, annoyance.
What picture do you have in your head about how the character is feeling when the text says (insert quote)?
What does the text show us about this character when it says (insert quote)?
What might this character be thinking when (insert quote)?

Misconception mapping: Pupils with limited vocabulary will struggle with emotive language. Come armed with vocabulary choices to describe the emotions behind each section in order to expand the ways the pupils can state an opinion.

Round up: Overall, how would you describe the impression this text gives about what is to come in the rest of the story? Do you think it will be a positive or negative series of events? Why do you think this?

Session 6: Making inferences with evidence from the text

Aims: To build up the ability to extract specific evidence linked to an understanding
    To identify the most fit-for-purpose evidence where more than one piece of evidence exists

Extract: Pages 50–65

Lesson content: Revisit the end of the previous section of text that the pupils read. Remind them of the opinion that was formed in session five. Think aloud and model how the evidence in the text proved that this opinion was accurate, e.g. 'We had said that Nicholas' mother felt a great sense of dread. If I wanted to prove that or justify that opinion, I need to revisit my text and pick out the best piece of evidence'. Model classifying evidence saying things like 'oh it says this…. yeah that's good but what if there is something better? Oh let me read on… OK here it is! Because the text says (insert best quote) and that is all I need – that definitely proves our opinion from the last sentence'. After this demonstration, revisit the process with the pupils. Ask them if they noticed what you did? Point out that you did not just read the first possibility but you read the whole section then picked out the best evidence. You did not include the whole sentence but a few grouped words that were specific evidence linked to your opinion.

Model the 'find and copy' question type, noting that you had to retrieve the exact words from the text. Also model a question type where you have to slightly vary the language for grammatical sense but stick as close as possible to the text details.

Key questions:

Find one piece of evidence that tells us X.

Identify two pieces of evidence that shows that X.

Use the 'Find and copy questioning approach to make pupils really narrow down evidence while also using their inference as well as vocabulary and meaning skills simultaneously, e.g. Find and copy the word that shows the character felt X. Find and copy the group of words that suggests that X. Find and copy two groups of words that imply X.

Misconception mapping: Look for pupils copying full sentences instead of phrases or poor word-meaning association. Use leading questions to help them refine responses, e.g. which words in that answer can be removed and the key detail is still kept? As this is a verbal reasoning session with pupils writing responses on boards, be prepared to repeat the questions clearly so pupils are able to refocus on whether they have answered accurately. Look for pupils copying one word where two words are the requisite response.

Summary: What skill did we use when identifying evidence? Did we always have to copy word for word from the text? What type of questions we did need to retrieve word for word answers for?

Year 6

Book used for sessions: *Holes* by Louis Sachar

Session 1: Making predictions and applying inference

Aim: To activate prior knowledge, make links to own experience, make links to texts and make links between pictures/objects

Resources: Pairs of pictures linked to characters and settings from the text; artefacts associated with the text, e.g. a shovel, an old weathered leather case

Lesson content: Discuss each picture or object in turn. Ask pupils what they think each picture or object is and what they know about them. How could each picture or object be connected to the story? Discuss any other stories that the pupils know to which the pictures or objects might be relevant.

Ask the pupils to put the items in pairs that they think are connected in meaning or that they think can be grouped together based on similarity. Encourage them to explain why they placed these items together. Finally, read and explore the book cover and blurb.

Key questions:

Why do you think the illustrator chose this picture/colour?
What do you know about X?
How do these link together?
What could the book be about? (Predict)
What does X mean in the blurb? (Vocabulary)
What type/genre of story is it? How do you know?
When do you think this story is taking place?
Have you seen the film based on this book?
What other things do you know about this time in history?

Round up: What was particularly strange about the camp?

Session 2: Identifying content and understanding its meaning

Aims: To pick up on the author's structure of language
To understand what meaning can be inferred by the text

Extract: Pages 3–10

Resources: Content lens poster or slide for the board

Lesson content: Read pages 1–10 of *Holes* by Louis Sachar. Use content lenses to visually demonstrate the difference between the sentence lengths. Ask the pupils what they notice the difference is between Chapter 1, 2 and 3. Discuss why the first two chapters were very short ones and discuss their purposes and varied viewpoints. Who is speaking to the reader and when? Discuss how writers often lay out text to convey a particular meaning or for a particular purpose and how that also includes the use of vocabulary and punctuation. Encourage pupils to look for anything out of the ordinary and question the reason behind it. Re-read each paragraph for the purpose of narrowing the focus of the pupils to target particular uses of vocabulary and punctuation.

Model scanning for unusual uses of punctuation, e.g. the hyphen and use of the dash on the first page. Discuss their purpose. Look closely at the use of inverted commas around *lake*. Deliberately use a sarcastic tone when reading 'lake' and ask if the pupils could pick up what the issue is and why the writer deliberately used inverted commas. Check to see if they recognise that it was not speech but that it actually shows that there is no lake present. Refer to the text evidence from the blurb read in the previous lesson.

Scan for deliberate sentence patterns on the second page of Chapter 1. Note the deliberate use of short sentences and the repetition of particular words. Discuss how this affects the tone of the text.

Move on to Chapter 3 one page at a time. Ask pupils to scan for deliberate uses of punctuation for meaning and to make notes independently on their whiteboards for discussion.

Key questions:

What does the information after the dash relate to?

What does *3:1* relate to in the text?

How does the hyphenated word look different to previous words with hyphens we have seen in chapter 1? Why is it deliberately written this way?

What impression do you get of the story about Stanley's great grandfather based on how his name is written?

How do you know there is a verse from a song on the following page? What is the name of this style of writing?

How are you meant to sing the word *moon*? How do you know? How does the writer's use of dashes change in this word from how it was used before?

Look at the use of inverted commas on page nine. Are they all used for speech? How are some used differently?

Why are there italics on the final page of the chapter? Are all the italics used in the same way? How are they different in meaning?

Misconception mapping: Scanning for punctuation and structure difference will reveal which pupils have gaps in their grammatical knowledge. Look out for pupils confusing hyphens and dashes and not seeing the elongated hyphenated compound as one word. Look for confusion around the use of inverted commas. Ensure there is clear understanding of the use of italics for emphasising, e.g. how *lucky* the character is as well as how they are used for quoting from the song.

Round up: Can the same punctuation be used in different ways for different meanings?

Session 3: Identifying choice of language and effect

Aim: To be able to sort language according to emotive impact depending on the mood it creates in the text

Extract: Pages 11–14

Resources: A mood lens and emotive lens poster or slide for the board

Lesson content: Explain to the pupils that writers deliberately choose vocabulary in order to affect the reader's understanding of the mood they wish to create – that mood is the atmosphere of a text which generates the reader's emotional response. Words, phrases and pictures can trigger either a positive or negative mood. By noting how the writer's deliberate use of language affects mood, pupils will be able to recognise the effect on a particular emotion.

Read the first page of the chapter and model noting words that affect mood; write these on the board in a chart with the headings positive and negative. Following which, create a summary mood by simply drawing a mood face which gives the general mood of the section of text on the board. Draw an emoji in this case to represent that Stan felt tense and uncomfortable, ensuring vocabulary goes beyond the basic 'sad' or 'nervous' examples of reader response. Instruct pupils to do the same exercise on the other pages, focusing on descriptions of the centre and its setting only. Ensure they avoid basic descriptions in order to be more specific. Gather responses and see if pupils are able to pick up on all positive or negative language. Pupils should also draw a mood face to summarise the mood of this section. Discuss findings and model appropriate emotions of the reader where needed. Advise that if there is no positive vocabulary it is because the writer is deliberately not using any in order to create a negative mood.

Key questions:

What kind of place was the detention centre? What do you 'see'?
What language did the writer use to give you this impression?
How did Stan feel while settling in? What examples can you provide that gave you this feeling?
Why did the writer use the name *Mr. Sir*? What impression does this give you about the guard?

Misconception mapping: Look for pupils sorting neutral language – where no emotion is implied – and ask them to describe the feeling in order for them to reflect on incorrect choices and improve them. Look for pupils only choosing words and no phrases; challenge and stretch them to sort at least two phrases. Look for pupils trying to deliberately find positive language where the mood of the text is negative.

Summary: What is the overall impression the writer wants to give the reader of the camp?

Session 4: Identifying and summarising main ideas

Aim: To enable re-telling of text

Extract: Pages 15–20

Resources: Whiteboards and pens

Lesson content: Recall the SOS strategy (p.88) and how it helps pupils to summarise. Explain to pupils that they will be writing statements that capture the main idea from more than one paragraph. Revisit prior learning about the main idea, capturing the subject character and the main event taking place. Model skimming the first page using the skimming strategy to pick up on the key details. Using set parameters (a specific number of words), summarise the first page as simply 'Stan met Mr. Pendanski'. Ask the pupils how else they could describe Mr Pendanski based on his role. Edit and improve their responses to say Stan met his counsellor. Explain the difference between the two answers in that the improved response gave the main idea a more significant detail of who Mr. Pendanski was.

Read the next paragraph and give the pupils a point of summary and a parameter, e.g. In three words, describe Mr. Pendanski's behaviour towards Stan. Continue working through the extract in this way, each time increasing the amount of text covered but keeping strict parameters on the statements to be written. Ensure there is a teacher model of a summary statement for each section of the text in case pupils struggle.

Misconception mapping: Look for pupils still copying vocabulary from the text – retrieving instead of summarising – and revisit the principles of SOS strategy.

Round up: Can we give one statement giving the main idea of the entire chapter we read today?

Session 5: Linking vocabulary to meaning

Aim: To sensitise pupils to the skill of scanning for language with a given meaning
To improve pupils' ability to copy as well as to apply previously taught vocabulary strategies

Extract: Pages 21–25

Resources: Whiteboards and pens

Lesson content: In this session, the teacher should present pupils with various word or phrase definitions and pupils will need to seek the text that links to the given understanding. This lesson mimics what often presents as comprehension-style questioning and removes the cognitive load of pupils having to write definition statements themselves. Discuss this type of 'find and copy' question and the various response requirements that come with this question type, e.g. they may need to copy a word, a group of words (a phrase) or more than one word not presented beside each other in a phrase. This ensures a greater degree of accuracy according to the question type.

On the board, write an example of a 'find and copy' question whose answer is just one word then ask children this question type three times for them to practise. Then increase in cognitive demand to more than one word and then a group of words. Model applying any of the 3Rs according to the language used in the question to ensure children are making use of previously learned strategies. Model checking that the question links to the section of the text through deliberate and explicit scanning. Collate responses from the children and get children to peer mark and feed back to each other on any misconceptions and how to use strategies to correct themselves.

Key questions:

Repeatedly ask pupils to 'find and copy' but systematically increase the level of challenge, like so:
Find and copy a word that tells us/that shows X.
Find and copy two words that tells us/that shows X.
Find a copy a phrase that tells us/that shows X.

Misconception mapping: Look for pupils struggling to scan for the right text evidence and also look for pupils who need the question repeated as they will need to hold the meaning of the word they are looking for in their memory. Repeat as needed but be aware that doing this makes it more cognitively challenging and means they replay the meaning in their heads rather than just having it on paper.

Round up: What strategies did you use to help figure out the meanings?

Session 6: Making inferences with evidence from the text

Aim: To apply the full P-chart (p.94)
  To provide fully developed and structured inference responses with justification

Extract: Pages 26–40

Resources: P-chart display

Lesson content: Revisit the P-chart equation and check for retention of the strategies for writing a fully developed answer. Explain that pupils will be using the full formula twice as they will be writing more developed answers, usually presented on several lines and worth three marks. For this session, one question will be modelled and one question will be answered with ample opportunity to edit and improve.

Write a question on the board and model a well-developed structured response while using the think-aloud process to make inference visible. Annotate where each part of the P-chart is evident in the answer to check that the cognitive steps were not missed.

Misconception mapping: Look for pupils missing cognitive steps or dropping the explanation of the evidence given. Look for pupils doing process once instead of twice.

Summary: Revisit the P-chart process and prompt editing and improving.

While these are just samples from upper KS2, similar formats have been used in lower and middle KS2 with the same success. The sessions give short burst strategy intervention and therefore the limit of text focus is brief and concentrated. The role of a group reading teacher is not to finish a whole book but to work with extracts that are rich, engaging and will have enough cognitive demand to challenge pupils and develop their understanding. Pupils should be encouraged to read books in totality outside of group reading – and often have a keen desire to do so. Chapter books are ideal for these sessions as it allows for full storylines to be explored within 30 minutes.

Group reading is an intervention model of teaching and should never replace whole-class teaching of comprehension nor should it be a long-term intervention. When pupils show metacognitive adherence to strategies, they are no longer in need of intervention and should return to only whole-class lessons. Group reading must be done with pupils who have similar gaps in understanding – meaning all pupils in the group are working at similar levels of attainment – in order for the gaps to be bridged effectively.

In this intimate setting, additional gaps will become evident and must drive the planning of the sessions as needed. There is no rush to plough through to other domains while pupils still show difficulties in grappling one. The beauty of group reading is that you get to know your readers' issues intricately, making you an effective enabler to bring these pupils to greater depth of understanding.

9 Pathways for planning comprehension effectively with rich KS2 texts

Effective planning of whole-class comprehension teaching is based on two phases. At the start of a block of teaching, there should be heavy focus on explicit modelling, scaffolding and skill-building questioning in order to build strong comprehension skills. Good planning must predict misconceptions to which teachers ought to be reactive. Being explicit in instruction from the onset should reduce time necessary for intervention, and practice must be given priority before engaging independent activities in Phase 1. By Phase 2, when readers are more confident in their knowledge and application of strategies, less explicit instruction is needed and practice time increases with strategy teaching acting as a reminder or support for those readers still in need of such. There will be a gradual release of instruction and intervention with increased independent capability by Phase 2. As such, when planning for Phase 1 lessons teachers should invest the majority of their time in identifying how the skill focus can be explicitly demonstrated by purposefully selecting text that demands the use of specific child-friendly strategies. Hence, strategy planning is the second priority focus of the planning phase.

In this section, you will find useful planning pathways for rich and diverse KS2 fiction texts using the systematic approach as a guide. The purpose of this section is not to break down the individual skills but to give a best fit flow of teaching in sequential order based on book content and how it connects to the testable reading domains. Notice that despite there being a suggested systematic order of teaching domain skills, it is within the power of the book to drive what is relevant and when. However, there still must be a systematic approach to ensure that at each step pupils are secure in the necessary strategies for further understanding the book. It is also not the intention of these pathways to dictate how long a teacher should spend on each chapter but to highlight the key learning intentions that can be excised from each chapter's content and show how strategies mentioned in this book can be easily integrated into everyday teaching. After all – what's a guide without planning support?

May the following be as helpful as it is intended.

Pig Heart Boy by Malorie Blackman

Chapter 1 – Content and meaning – The layout of this chapter is loaded with structure deliberately manipulated for meaning. There is an abundance of short sentences, repetition and the entire chapter is in in italics and the ellipses are varied in usage.

Chapter 2 – Choice of language and effect – Content and meaning overlaps in this chapter. However, there is an abundance of figurative language, i.e. similes and personification, to explore the effect on the reader, simple vocabulary is executed with deliberate shades of meaning and there are many colloquialisms to grapple with. By the end of this chapter, vocabulary becomes higher levelled with some technical words coming through. The final two lines feature an interesting use of onomatopoeia which will need rich discussion with regards to the author's intended effect.

Chapter 3 – Vocabulary –The pupils will make much use of vocabulary strategies in this chapter. There is challenging vocabulary and meaty phrases to explore, some of which will benefit from background knowledge exploration regarding the use of a pig's heart for a human transplant.

Chapter 4 – Inference and justification –Vocabulary and choice of language skills will greatly influence each reader's ability to infer in this chapter. Viewpoints and ideals will need to be fully explored before pupils can infer. Sorting different perspectives is useful for this chapter to be fully understood through exploring the emotions behind each character's response to the main event. This chapter demands empathy and will deliver rich inferences both through discussion and justification.

Chapter 5 – Comparison – This chapter is perfect for the teaching of comparisons as contrasts can be made both between the main character and his best friend's attitudes as well as comparing who had similar attitudes to the main character's mother or father.

Chapter 6 – Retrieval – Chapter 6 is filled with newness: new settings and new characters with a lot of detailed descriptions. It is therefore perfect for the teaching of retrieval.

Chapter 7 – Summarising – This is a relatively short chapter but there is a lengthy dialogue which lends itself to summarising well and chunkier paragraphs for practising sorting key details to determine the main ideas based on the main character's emotions.

Chapter 8 – Skills Overlap: Content and Meaning, Choice of language and effect – Chapter 8 has wonderful examples of the deliberate manipulation of font for meaning. Pupils will see examples of informal and formal dialogue which all builds character depth.

Chapter 9 – Skills overlap: Prediction and Inference – Chapter 9 is a very emotional one which features a poem written by the main character. There are many opportunities to infer, justify and by the end predict the character's purpose of the chapter with the key questions *'What does Cameron think may happen to him? What is his reason for making this recording?'*

The House with Chicken Legs by Sophie Anderson

Pages 1–24 – Retrieval – This section of the text lends itself well to identifying key details. Filled with subject specific vocabulary, pupils have the opportunity to practice scanning for meaning using the glossary (overlapping with content and meaning). There are plenty of unfamiliar settings and context to explore as they get to know the characters and cultural references introduced. Retrieval will help pupils navigate through the new magical world.

Pages 25–38 – Inference and prediction – A new experience of friendship opens up many emotions for the main character. There are ample opportunities to infer and develop emotive language in this section. It also allows for several forward inferences (predictions) which can be revisited later.

Pages 39–47 – Choice of language and effect – Figurative language and phrases of interest are used in this short chapter. It is a good extract to move pupils on to focus on the effect of groups of words as opposed to individual words.

Pages 48–60 – Vocabulary and meaning – Some tricky use of simple vocabulary lends itself well to applying the read around strategy. There are a few challenging words and several personified phrases to explore, overlapping with choice of language and effect.

Pages 61–71 – Content and meaning – This chapter features four sections all divided using stylistics. This provides an opportunity to explore the writer's use of sections and their purpose. There is also a deliberate juxtaposition of light and darkness and several opportunities to apply content lenses.

Pages 71–82 – Summarising – As a new character is introduced, pulling out significant details and annotating main ideas will be useful in this section. The paragraphs are meaty and well suited for pupils in Phase 2 of teaching this skill. The SOS strategy will enable them to develop succinct statements as they practice summarising.

Pages 83–91 – Skills overlap: Vocabulary and meaning with content and meaning – An excellent chapter for examining the overlapping of two domains. The vocabulary present here is challenging and several subject-specific words are used beyond those listed in the glossary. There are also varied uses of italics to be explored. This is well-suited for Phase 2 of the teaching of both skills where the 3Rs strategy and use of content lenses are already established.

Pages 92–101 – Comparison – An inner conflict of emotions for the main character provides great teaching moments where her thoughts and actions can be compared. This chapter lends itself well to comparing across sections of text and using mood lenses will support the understanding of emotive changes in character behaviour.

Letters from the Lighthouse by Emma Carroll

Chapter 1, pages 1–4 – Choice of language and effect – Several examples of shades of meaning to be explored including figurative language, colloquialism and compound words deliberately designed for effect on pages 1 and 2. Similes are used for character depth on page 3 and there are personification examples to explore on page 4.

Chapter 1, pages 5–13 – Skills overlap: Content and meaning with inference – The use of font manipulation for meaning is significant in the remaining pages of this chapter. Pupils can explore italics, capitals, uses of dashes with a variety of meanings. There is a lot of onomatopoeic language. Content lenses for both word and sentence levels should be used here to pull out the moods of language and aid in inferring character feelings based on events.

Chapter 2 – Inference and justification – An excellent chapter to apply the systematic approach to building up pupils' ability to justify. A highly emotive chapter where the mood lens can be applied to develop deeper discussions around the interactions between the characters gleaned through dialogue and action from pages 1–18. Overlap with more content and meaning from page 19–22, where ellipses and italics take on additional meanings (refer to content lenses as needed).

Chapter 3, pages 25–30 – Retrieval – As there are many new characters and events introduced in this chapter, it is an ideal one for retrieving significant detail. On page 30, draw attention to the use of the dinkus and question its purpose to ensure pupils are holding their content focus.

Chapter 3, pages 30–32 – Vocabulary and meaning – These pages provides good opportunity to revisit the 3Rs with some challenging vocabulary used. There is also some technical vocabulary where background knowledge will need to be planted/activated.

Chapter 4, pages 33–44 – Summarising – Several shorter paragraphs in this chapter makes it ideal for Phase 1 of summarising main ideas. The events are fast paced and detailed with plenty of opportunity to encourage application of the SOS strategy. Do round up with sequencing the events using summarised statements.

Chapter 5 – Comparison – This chapter presents various settings and new characters which can be juxtaposed with those from previous chapters. It is an ideal opportunity to explore what is different and what is similar especially when focusing on the protagonist's and antagonist's personalities.

Chapter 6, pages 55–64 – Multi-domain layers – Ideal for using layered questioning for all domains areas. It presents good opportunities for vocabulary strategies, shades of meaning and effect on the reader, several examples for use of content lenses and even includes different genres of text (postcard and mystery code) to explore. The change of moods provide ample basis for inference and justification. This is a key chapter for the independent application of skills during the gradual release phase (Phase 2).

After the War by Tom Palmer

Chapter 1 – Prediction and inference – There are several opportunities for the pupils to make forward inferences in this chapter with the author's repeated use of rhetorical questions. Certainly, suspend readings to explore the impact of these questions on the thoughts of the reader. Round up the chapter with some retrieval of key details about the characters introduced.

Chapter 2 – Choice of language and effect – This chapter features opportunities to use the 'sketch what you see' strategy to pull out understanding. There are several word choices deliberately used to intensify meaning for the pupils to determine their effect on the reader using emotive language.

Chapter 3 – Vocabulary and meaning – While there is some subject-specific vocabulary you will need to inform the pupils of, there is ample opportunity to use the 3Rs strategy to clarify meaning in this chapter. There is challenging vocabulary as well as simple vocabulary used differently where reading around the word will be the most important strategy.

Chapter 4 – Skills overlap: Content and meaning with Inference and justification – Sentence-level content lenses can be applied in this chapter as pupils work through techniques used by the writer to build tension as well as the purpose of the use of the multiple dinkuses.

Chapter 5 – Skills overlap: Inference and justification with comparison – A meaty chapter filled with emotional twists perfect for the systematic approach to inference and building up justification. With a new setting introduced in this chapter, this is an opportunity to compare descriptions and emotions from previous chapters. Do ensure the 3Rs are well applied through vocabulary priming to fully clarify meaning of some tricky vocabulary in this chapter before questioning around inference.

Chapter 6 – Summarising – Perfect for practicing the SOS strategy around events, dialogue and descriptions. Pupils can pull out key details and annotate as well as sequence main idea statements.

Chapter 7 – Multi-domain layers – This chapter is ideal for revisiting several skills in Phase 2 of teaching. Vocabulary strategies should be fully embedded by this chapter to enable independent application of the 3Rs. Do vary question types for retrieval, vocabulary, inference and justification, content and meaning and choice of language for this section and use this as an opportunity to teach different question styles for pupils to then independently respond.

The Other Side of Truth by Beverley Naidoo

Chapter 1 – Content and meaning – Filled with several stylistics for effect, as pupils immerse themselves into the characters and setting do explore the purpose of italics, ellipses and inverted commas. The use of the content lenses will be purposeful here; be sure to address the deliberate shaping of paragraphs where extra breaks are taken to indicate movement of time.

Chapter 2 – Retrieval – A brief chapter with key details to explore which are pivotal to the book's development. An ideal opportunity to use the strategy of striking off supporting detail and noting significant information in Phase 1 of teaching.

Chapter 3 – Inference and justification – An emotive chapter ideal for working on inference and justification. Its reflective nature is ideal for pupils to practise writing more structured and developed inference responses using the P-chart, as vocabulary is very accessible.

Chapter 4 – Vocabulary and meaning – An ideal chapter for fully applying the 3Rs, building up synonym language for clarifying meaning and explaining understanding. Perfect for Phase 2 of vocabulary teaching.

Chapter 5 – Choice of language and effect – With lots of mood-enhancing vocabulary used by the writer, this chapter is best suited to exploring shades of words and phrases. Using the mood lens to determine positive and negative nuances will enable pupils to infer meanings beyond the text evidence.

Chapter 6 – Summarising – A very short chapter for a quick practice of the SOS strategy in Phase 1 of teaching. Pupils can ideally highlight key details and annotate main statements. It is also an opportunity to teach a summary style of question for pupils to practise responding to.

Chapter 7 – Comparison – A change of setting with stark differences to the origin of the main character and family. This is a perfect opportunity to compare scenes and character emotions.

Chapter 8 – Skills overlap: Inference and justification with content and meaning – Many implications in this chapter mean it lends itself well to inference. This is an ideal section of text to practise justifying opinions by finding the best fit evidence to prove or disprove a given statement. There are some stylistics (italics and punctuation for effect) to be explored.

10 Conclusion: Bringing it together

The mastery approach to teaching reading removes the fast pace of going through text in a way that leaves misconceptions missed. It prevents the gaps in pupils' ability to understand language from widening. By ensuring we are systematic and explicit, we effectively remove instances of cognitive overload. Likewise, by teaching strategies linked to the domains we arm our pupils with useful and effective means to drive their own learning and tackle any problems they come across – not only through questioning but within their own minds as readers. Mastery evolves comprehension beyond the point of discussion to written visible progress allowing pupils to demonstrate in depth their connections to text. The beauty of teaching in this way has proven to be the most fruitful pedagogical practice teachers trained in mastery have used to date and their reward is simply seeing every child take away meaningful knowledge from whatever book they access.

While this book is mostly about KS2 practice, KS1 can certainly benefit from the mastery approach. Recently I was involved with this being introduced successfully to 90 pupils in Year 2 whose teachers now use the mastery principles with full effect, transforming whole-school practice and, most importantly, improving achievement for their pupils. These works will be reflected in the complementary website (www.readmaster.co.uk) in order to build cohesion across both KS1 and KS2.

There are several references to strategies and resources that are a starting point for the mastery approach in this book. The accompanying website will provide teachers with an even greater insight into how to embed this approach on a day-to-day basis, making resources, strategies mentioned and newly developed ones easily accessible. The teaching materials on the site will include demo videos, full units of learning to cover the KS2 year with downloadable slides, strategy cards and icons matched to rich texts. ReadMaster as a planning platform will follow the systematic approach explored in this book that will result in rigorous teaching which empowers children to make their comprehension visible while removing workload pressures and assuring quality first teaching.

I truly hope this book and the supplementary website will provide the complete support teachers need. And remember…

"It is better to know one book intimately than a hundred superficially."

– Donna Tartt, *The Secret History*

Bibliography

Allan Poe, E. (2016), *The Raven*. New York: Abrams.

Anderson, S. (2018), *The House with Chicken Legs*. London: Usborne Publishing Ltd.

Blackman, M., (2011), *Pig Heart Boy*. Great Britain: The Random House Group Ltd.

Bloom, B. (1966) *Taxonomy of Educational Objectives, Handbook I: The Cognitive Domain*. USA: David McKay Company.

Broek, P. ven den, (1990), 'The Causal Inference Maker: Towards a Process of Inference Generation in Text Comprehension'. In: Balota, D.A., Flores d'Arcais and Rayner, K. (eds) *Comprehension Process in Reading*. New Jersey: Lawrence Erlbaum Associates, Inc.

Brooks, G., (2002), *What works for children with literacy difficulties? The effectiveness of intervention schemes: Research report RR380*. England: Department for Education and Skills.

Bryan, T.A., (2019), *The Art of Comprehension*. USA: Stenhouse Publishers.

Bunzl, P., (2016), *Cogheart*. London: Usborne Publishing Ltd.

Carroll, E. (2017), *Letters from the Lighthouse*. London: Faber & Faber Limited.

Chambers, A., (2011), *Tell Me: Children, Reading & Talk with the Reading Environment*. UK: The Thimble Press.

CLPE (2019), *Reflecting realities: Survey of ethnic representation within UK children's literature 2018*.

CLPE (2020), *What we know works booklets*, https://clpe.org.uk/library-and-resources/what-we-know-works-booklets.

Cremin, T., Mottram, M., Collins, F.M., Powell, S. and Safford, K., (2014), *Building Communities of Engaged Readers*. Oxon: Routledge.

Dahl, R., (1995), *Charlie and the Chocolate Factory*. London: Puffin Books.

DfE (2013), *English programmes of study: key stages 1 and 2, National Curriculum in England*. London: Crown.

DfE, Education standards research team (2012), *Research evidence on reading for pleasure*. London: Crown.

Doherty, B. (2009), *Street Child*. London: HarperCollins Children's Books.

DWP, Social Justice and Disadvantaged Groups Division (2012), *Social justice: transforming lives*. London: Crown.

Edge, C., (2016), *The Many Worlds of Albie Bright*. London: Nosy Crow Ltd.

Education Endowment fund, (2018), *Teaching & Learning Toolkit*, https://educationendowmentfoundation.org.uk/evidence-summaries/teaching-learning-toolkit/reading-comprehension-strategies/technical-appendix/.

Fisher, D., & Frey, N. (2008). *Better learning through structured teaching: A framework for the gradual release of responsibility* (p. 4). Alexandria, VA: ASCD.

Flesch, R. (1951), *How to Test Readability*. New York: Harper and Brothers.

Gavin, J., (2014), *Blackberry Blue and other fairy tales*. UK: Penguin Random House.

Greder, A. (2008), *The Island*. London: Allen & Unwin.

Hodgson Burnette, F (1911)., *The Secret Garden* – eBook, Chapter 1, viewed May 2020, http://www.authorama.com/secret-garden-1.html.

Howell, A.M. (2020), *The House of One Hundred Clocks*. London: Usborne Publishing Ltd.

Lawton, K. and Warren, H., (2015) *The Power of Reading: How the next government can unlock every child's potential through reading*. London: Save the Children on behalf of the Read On. Get On. campaign.

McKay, H, (2001), *Saffy's Angel*. Great Britain: Hodder Children's Books.

Miller, D. (2009), *The Book Whisperer: Awakening the Inner Reader in Every Child*. San Francisco, CA: Jossey- Bass.

Murray, S. (2020), *Orphans of the Tide*. London: Penguin Random House Children's.

Naidoo, B., (2017), *The Other Side of Truth*. London: Penguin Random House Children's.

Norriss, A. (2006), *The Unluckiest Boy in the World*. London: Penguin Books Ltd

Palacio, R.J., (2014), *Wonder*. London: Random House Children's Publisher

Palacio, R.J.,(2012), *Wonder FAQ*, Viewed 18th June 2020, https://rjpalacio.tumblr.com/post/36554274751/wonder-faqs.

Palmer, Tom, (2020), *After the War*. Edinburgh: Barrington Stoke Ltd.

Piaget, J. and Inhelder, B. (1969), *The Psychology of the Child*. New York: Basic Books.

Pieper, K. (2016), *How to Teach Reading for Pleasure*. Wales: Independent Thinking Press.

Raphael, T. and Au, K., (2005), 'QAR: Enhancing Comprehension and Test Taking Across Grades and Content Areas'. In: *Reading Teacher – READ TEACH*. 59. 206–221. 10.1598/RT.59.3.1.

Rasheed, L. (2020), *Empire's End – A Roman Story*. London: Scholastic Children's Books

Rasinski, T.V. and Cheesman Smith, M. (2018), *The Megabook of Fluency: Strategies and Texts to Engage All Readers*. USA: Scholastic Inc.

Raúf, O.Q. (2019), *The Star Outside My Window*. UK: Hachette Children's Group.

Reutzel, D.R., (2011), Organising Effective Literacy Instruction: Differentiating Instruction to Meet Student Needs". In: Mandel Morrow, L and Gambrell, L.B. (eds.) (2011), *Best Practices in Literacy Instruction: Fourth Edition*. New York: The Guilford Press.

Robinson, W.P. and Rackstraw, S.J., (1975), *Questioning and answering skills in school children*. Sydney: Macquarie University, 11–15, https://files.eric.ed.gov/fulltext/ED143418.pdf.

Sachar, L. (1998), *Holes*. London: Bloomsbury Publishing.

Scarborough, H. S. (2001), 'Connecting early language and literacy to later reading (dis)abilities: Evidence, theory, and practice'. In: S. Neuman & D. Dickinson (eds), *Handbook for research in early literacy*. New York, NY: Guilford Press.

Smith, M. and Turner, J., (2016), *The common European framework of reference for Languages (CEFR) and the Lexile® Framework for Reading*, located at https://metametricsinc.com/wp-content/uploads/2018/01/CEFR_1.pdf

STA (2018), *2019 key stage 2 English reading booklet*. London: Crown.

Standards and Testing Agency (2015), *2016 Key stage 2 English reading test framework: National Curriculum tests from 2016*. England: STA.

Standards Testing Agency (2018), *Assessment and reporting arrangements (ARA) key stage 2 2019*. England: STA.

Tartt, D., (1992), *The Secret History*. London: Penguin Group, p.32.

Taylor, T., (2019), *Malamander*. London: Walkers Books Ltd.

This isn't included in the text anywhere.

Trask, R. L., (1997), *The Penguin Guide to Punctuation*. London: Penguin Books Ltd.

Tyng, C.M, Amin, H.U, Saad, M.N.M and Malik, A.S., (2017), 'The Influences of Emotion on Learning and Memory', *Frontiers in Psychology*, Volume 8: Article 1454.

Williamson, V., (2018), *The Fox Girl and the White Gazelle*. Edinburgh: Floris Books.

Index

Note: Page numbers in *italics* denote figures.

3D items, use of 18–19
3Rs strategy, for vocabulary and meaning 80–1
   read around the word strategy 81–2
   replace the word strategy 84, 95
   root word strategy 82–3

action 12
activating/planting background knowledge 17
   drip-feed intermittent knowledge
      enhancement 19–20
   examples
     how many questions? 22
     match the images 22–3
     mystery in a box 21
     silent annotation 20
     sketch what you 'see' 24–7
   practical ideas 19–20
   pre-read priming of knowledge 19–20
   'what can I bring to life' 18–19
     examples 22–7
   'what is completely new' 18
     example 22
   'what we should already know' 17
     examples 20–1, 22–7
analytical skills 113
attainment in comprehension 3, 5–6

background knowledge awareness, usage in text
      selection 16–17
   see also activating/planting knowledge
backward inference 36
Bloom's taxonomy 8, 61
book talk 13
book talk-ability 13, 72–4
book talk-ability questioning 72–4
   sample 123–36
Brooks, Greg 2
Bryan, Trevor Andrew 92, 115

clarity 5
close copy strategy 103
coherence inference 36
collaborative learning 7

collaborative marking 62
comparison, testable domain 42–4
compound words 83
confirmation 62
content and meaning, testable domain 38–40
   ability to decode 114
   language patterns 114
   punctuation recognition 114
content lenses *115*, 115–16
   emotive lenses 122, *122*
   guide to 116–21
   language lenses choice 121–2
   mood lenses 121, ***122***
Cremin, Teresa 6, 13

diverse texts, access to 7
drama 41
drip-feed intermittent knowledge
      enhancement 19–20

eight wonders of teaching 9–13, *10*
elaborative inference 36
enunciation 5
evidence, and inference 99
explicit skills instruction 14
expression 5, 12

find and copy strategy 88
Flesch reading ease score 7
fluency 5
forward inference 36

gap analysis 7
global inference 36
gradual release 79
grammar 113
group reading intervention 88
group-reading intervention model *123*
guided questioning 66, 71–2

independent thinking aloud 75, 76, 78
inference and justification 36–7, 52, 54
   inference types 36

mastery of inferring using evidence 109–11
mastery of justification 105–6
processing chart 93–9
strategy 92–3
systematic teaching guidance for inference 99–104
TAFE process 37
written responses for justification strategy,
    structuring of 93–9
invitational thinking aloud 75–6, 77–8

justification *see* inference and justification

Kispal, Anne 36
'knowings' 15
knowledge-based question 56–8

language
    ability to decode 114
    bringing to life 19
    choice, and its effect 40–2
    components, illustration of *113*
    and punctuation 115
lenses strategy 92–3
    see also content lenses
lexical grammatical complexities 7
lexico-grammatical density 51
Lexile framework 51
local inference 36

mastery, definition of 3
Miller, Donalyn 13
misconception 102–3, 143
    and guided questioning 71
    mapping 7–8, 61–2

narrative texts, and content manipulation 38
negative language 41
neutral language 41

opinions, and inference 99
oracy 41
own understanding, demonstration of 107–9

patterns in text and effect 113–14
P-chart *see* processing chart (P-chart)
performance play 41
persistent assessment 61
phonics 2, 5
Piaget's schema 15

pitch 5, 12
planning pathways 137
    After the War (Palmer) 140–1
    House with Chicken Legs, The (Anderson) 138–9
    Letters from the Lighthouse (Carroll) 139–40
    Other Side of Truth, The (Naidoo) 141–2
    Pig Heart Boy (Blackman) 137–8
poetry, and content manipulation 38
positive language 41
positive reinforcement 62
prediction, testable domain 36, 38
prefixed words 83
pre-reading 9
pre-read priming of knowledge 19–20
pre-teaching strategies 79
prior learning 16–17
prior texts 17
probing reading, teacher as the model of 66
processing chart (P-chart) 93–9
    repairing structure using 102–4
    structuring written responses using 99–102
punctuation 115
    recognition of 114
    significance in content and meaning 38
purposeful selection of text 10

Question-Answer Relationship (QAR) framework 64–5
questioning 61–2
    and actively integrating and assimilating
        information 63
    Bloom's taxonomy approach 61
    book talk-ability 72–4, 123–36
    collating the evidence 64
    differentiation through 66–9
    disposition to acquire knowledge 63
    efficient action 64
    evaluating and deciding 64
    extracting, defining and classifying the problems 63–4
    framework *61*
    guided questioning 66, 71–2
    making the inside outside 74–8
    and problem solving 63
    question and response relationship chart 65, *65*
    question-answer relationship 63, *63*, 64–5
    question type recognition strategies 63–5
    ramping up methodology 64, *64*, *67*, 67–70, **70**
    and response structure 64–5
    scaffolded questioning 66, *67*
    test purpose enquiry 66

ramping up methodology 64, *64*, *67*, 67–70, *70*
read around the word strategy 81–2
reading
    for attainment 5–6
    changes 1
    essentiality 1
    for pleasure 1, 2, 5–6
reading aloud 11–12, 41, 66
reading teaching 5, 9–13, *10*, 143
    fluency 5
    gradual release phase 30, 64, *64*
    introductory (scaffolding) phase 30, 64, *64*, 66
    pace of 9
    phases 30, 64
    providing equal access to rich and diverse texts 7
    pupils as readers, knowing about 6
    range of practice 8
    reading ahead of the class 9
    reading for pleasure versus reading for
        attainment 5–6
    teachers' knowledge of children's books 6
    valuing of practice as investigative reasoning 8–9
reasoning and wondering aloud 11, 74–5, *75*
replace the word strategy 84, 95
response zones 54–7
retrieval of information 33–4
    strategies 84
        find and copy strategy 87–8
        for group reading intervention 88
        scanning strategy 86–7
        skimming strategy 85–6
        SOS strategy 88–92
        strike-off strategy 84–5
root word strategy 82–3
RPAF audit 10

SATs test, mark allocation 29–30
scaffolded questioning 66, 67
scanning strategy 86–7
shades of meaning 41
skimming 33, 85–6
social media 2
SOS strategy 88–92
Standards and Testing Agency 29
steady building of skills 14
strategies 7–8
strategy planning 137
strategy teaching 79

systematic approach 80
    vocabulary and meaning strategies 80–1
subject knowledge 13–14
subject-specific technical language 57
suffixed words 83
summarising, testable domain 34–5

targeted layered approach 66
target information
    accessibility of 50–1
    complexity of 51
testable domains 14, 29
    comparison 42–4
    content and meaning 38–40
    inference and justification 36–7
    language choice and its effect 40–2
    order of teaching 44–5, *45*
    prediction 36, 38
    retrieval 33–4
    skills progression map 46–7
    summarising 34–5
    vocabulary and meaning 31–2
test frameworks 49
    cognitive demand of questions 49
        accessibility of the target information 50–1
        complexity of the target information 51
        response strategy 54–7
        task-specific complexity 51–4
        technical knowledge 57–60
test purpose enquiry 66
text selection, using background knowledge
        awareness in 16–17
thinking aloud
    independent thinking aloud 75, 76, 78
    invitational thinking aloud 75–6, 77–8
'think like a child' approach 15–16, 17
Trask, R. L. 114

visible comprehenders 3, 5, 79
visualisation of text 92
vocabulary and meaning 31–2
    strategies 80–1
        read around the word strategy 81–2
        replace the word strategy 84, 95
        root word strategy 82–3

written responses 79
    structuring using P-chart 99–102

Mastery resources for classroom practice

If you're looking for even more practical ideas and strategy resources for improving children's reading comprehension in KS2, check out the new planning platform ReadMaster.co.uk. You'll find systematic lesson plans including editable PowerPoint teaching slides you can adapt for your whole class reading text, key activity resources, and 'how to teach' demo videos.

With your smartphone or tablet, simply scan the QR code below for a FREE 7 day trial to access a wealth of further content on the mastery approach using quality KS2 texts from a variety of children's authors from the UK and internationally.

Check out the free bonus reading for pleasure videos and resources from The Author's Voice also available at ReadMaster.co.uk/signup.